MINDS
MADE FOR
STORIES

MINDS
MADE FOR
STORIES

How We **Really**
Read and Write
Informational and
Persuasive Texts

THOMAS
NEWKIRK

HEINEMANN
Portsmouth, NH

Heinemann
361 Hanover Street
Portsmouth, NH 03801–3912
www.heinemann.com

Offices and agents throughout the world

Credits continue on page vi.

Library of Congress Cataloging-in-Publication Data
Newkirk, Thomas.
  Minds made for stories : how we really read and write informational and persuasive texts / Thomas Newkirk.
       pages cm
  Includes bibliographical references.
  ISBN: 978-0-325-04695-2
  1. English language—Rhetoric—Study and teaching—United States.
2. English language—Composition and exercises—Study and teaching—United States. 3. Narration (Rhetoric)—Study and teaching—United States. 4. Language arts—United States.   I. Title.
PE1405.U6.N495 2014
808—dc23   2014015342

Editor: Margaret LaRaia
Production: Victoria Merecki
Cover and interior designs: Suzanne Heiser
Front cover photo: © Garry Gay/The Image Bank/Getty Images
Typesetter: Valerie Levy, Drawing Board Studios
Manufacturing: Steve Bernier

Printed in the United States of America on acid-free paper
18 17 16 15 14 VP 1 2 3 4 5

CONTENTS

Credits continued from page iv:

"Rules of Notice" from *Before Reading: Narrative Conventions and the Politics of Interpretation* by Peter J. Rabinowitz. Copyright © 1998. Published by Ohio State University Press. Reprinted by permission of the author.

Excerpts from *Biology: The Dynamics of Life*, California Student Edition, by Alton Biggs et al. Copyright © 2005 by McGraw Hill Education. Reprinted by permission of the publisher.

Figure 6.1: Copyright © Knorre / Shutterstock.

Figure 8.3: From "Population Projections" by Jeffrey Passel and D'Vera Cohn (2008). Pew Research Center, Washington, D.C. http://www.pewhispanic .org /2008/02/11/ii-population-projections/, accessed March 25, 2014. Reprinted by permission.

Figure 8.5: From Cancer Research UK. http://www.cancerresearchuk.org/cancer -info/cancerstats/types/lung/incidence/uk-lung-cancer-incidence-statistics #trends, accessed March 25, 2014. Reprinted by permission.

Figure 8.6: ASH Fact Sheet: "Smoking Statistics—Who Smokes and How Much" by Action on Smoking and Health (UK), October 2013. http://ash.org.uk/files /documents/ASH_106.pdf, accessed March 25, 2014. Reprinted by permission.

Figure 8.7: Wind Map (2012) by Martin M. Wattenberg and Fernanda Viegas from http://www.bewitched.com/windmap.html. Excerpts from http://hint.fm/about/. Reprinted by permission of the authors/designers.

ACKNOWLEDGMENTS

I remember with mortification my first meeting with Peter Elbow, who figures so prominently in this book. He came to the University of New Hampshire to give a talk, and I picked him up at Logan Airport. On the ride, he asked me about student writing at UNH. I launched into a description of how students were stymied by trying to be too formal, and they needed the chance to just let the writing flow like talk, without any worry about correctness. So I had them do nonstop writing for about ten minutes at the beginning of each class.

I presented these observations as if they were truly and originally my own. I was passionate. But suddenly, as I reached Portsmouth, I had a flash—I'd learned all of this from Peter Elbow, the man sitting beside me, who was graciously nodding his head, as if I was telling him something new.

My advisor James Kinneavy once remarked that his original ideas were those for which he'd forgotten the source. So true for me. So let me here acknowledge those I can't acknowledge by name, whose ideas became so much a part of my thinking that it seems like me own. I know you're out there.

But the book draws on three men who have shaped my thinking. The first, is, clearly Peter Elbow, whose most recent book *Vernacular Eloquence* (2012) is a crowning achievement in a career of innovation and creative thought.

As in so much of my work, I draw on the work of Don Murray, mentor, friend, colleague, and breakfast companion. His claims for narrative as a foundational writing mode gave me confidence that I might be on the right track.

appreciation

Occasionally we read a book that fundamentally alters our thinking. There is a before-and-after quality to the experience of the reading. This is the case for me with Daniel Kahneman's *Thinking, Fast and Slow* (2011). He demonstrates, beyond any doubt, that we are narrative creatures—always asking, "What's the story?"

I have greatly benefited from my work with *Educational Leadership*, which published a piece where I tried out the argument of this book. So many thanks to Amy Azzam and the staff there.

I inflicted a very early version of this chapter on several graduate students who gave me good feedback. Thanks to Marino Fernandes, Shawn Kelly, Amy Sauber, and Xiaoqiong You. I also received help on the "Seven Deadly Sins" chapter from Jon Bromley and Chris Hall. Adele Pulitzer provided me with children's science magazines.

As with all of my writing, I get to try out the ideas with the consultants of the Learning Through Teaching Program: Louise Wrobleski, Tomasen Carey, Penny Kittle, Terry Moher, Shirley Smith, Lisa Miller, Pam Mueller, Kathy Collins, Ellie Papazoglou, Marianne Ramsey. Thanks for your forbearance and help. Sabina Foote, as always, helped in compiling the manuscript into readable form at various points.

I was very fortunate to have encouraging readers along the way: Gerald Graff and Jonathan Lovell at the proposal stage; Katie Ray, Lad Tobin, Katherine Bomer, Penny Kittle, Jack Wilde, Maja Wilson, and Ellin Keene on the fuller manuscript. My primary reader and chief encourager was my editor Margaret LaRaia—I so appreciate that she was on my wavelength all the way.

I owe a debt to the wonderful Heinemann design and production staff. To Suzanne Heiser for her brilliance at interior and cover design; to Anthony Marvullo for his help with permissions; and to Victoria Merecki for keeping the final stages of the project on the rails. Thanks also to Kim Cahill of marketing and to Cindy Black for the copyediting (sorry I provided you with so many absent page numbers!).

Finally, there is my own father, a biologist, for whom science was alive, a romance. His is the voice always at my shoulder, urging me on.

PART 1

STAY
WITH
ME

informative

thought

metaphor

presence

CH 1 SUSTAINED READING

It avails not, neither time or place—distance avails not: I am with you, you men and women of a generation, or ever so many generations hence; I project myself—also I return—I am with you and know how it is.

WALT WHITMAN, "CROSSING BROOKLYN FERRY"

Our theories are really disguised autobiographies, often rooted in childhood. That is the case with this book—and I'll begin with two stories.

I grew up with a biologist father, actually an entomologist. He was the county expert on bugs. Sometimes we would get a call from a local Ohio farmer who had an insect for him to identify, so we would travel to Red Haw or Savannah to see a giant cecropia moth or luna butterfly or one of the six hundred species of Ohio spiders like the marbled orb weaver.

During World War II, he had been stationed in the Pacific where he gave soldiers lectures on quinine, which protected them from malaria— and he began research on his lifelong interest: mosquitoes. When we asked him if he was ever in any danger from being shot, he told us about wandering past the perimeter of his base, in search of some type of mosquito, and almost being shot by his own troops as he returned to camp (not exactly the war story we, as kids, were looking for).

After the war, as a college professor, he studied insects that preyed on mosquitoes. Every summer day he would strap on his army knapsack, call to our dachshund and head to Moss Hill, a wooded area near our house.

As he walked through the shaded woods, he had the uncanny ability to focus on the ends of twigs where he could notice a dance fly or a robber fly with its hind legs wrapped around an insect. He would close a empty peanut butter jar around the insect, shake its prey lose and release it, later classifying prey by order (Diptera, Lepidoptera, Coleoptera, etc.). Science in our house was never a dull set of facts; it was alive and fascinating.

Many of my dad's favorite science writers conveyed such a quality of attention and fascination that it felt like literature, the most notable example being Henri Fabre, the author of *The Insect World*. Fabre defiantly refused to write in the academic style of official science. He even evokes the insects themselves to testify in his behalf:

> *Come here, one and all of you—you, the stingbearers, and you, the wing-cased armour-clads—take up defence and bear witness in my favour. Tell of the intimate terms in which I live with you, of the patience with which I observe you, of the care with which I record your actions. Your evidence is unanimous: yes, my pages, though they bristle not with hollow formulas and learned smatterings, are the exact narrative of facts observed, neither more, nor less.*
> (1913/1964, 17)

That's the form of science I knew as a child.

My second story involves time. As humans we live *in time*, we sense our existence as a progression. Without this sense of the comprehensible passage of time, we are deeply disoriented. A few years ago, I was reminded how essential this time-sense is to our normal functioning. My mother, in her early 90s, developed a form of dementia where she could not locate herself in time. She would wake up in the morning and not be sure if the day was ending or beginning. All her life she had been an exact punctual woman, but she had no idea if she had missed hair or doctor appointments, if it was morning or afternoon.

My brother tried to help by buying large clocks that she could put around her apartment, but it didn't work because she had lost the capacity to translate 3:00 into the flow of a day. The effect on her was sheer panic, disorientation, to the point where she would wake up in the night and shriek.

Dementia, as we all know, can also take another form of time loss, and did for her. Although she could remember her phone number from the 1920s when it was first installed in her Ohio birthplace, she could not hold onto more recent events. Had she seen *Godfather II* or not? Had she taken her medicine or not? Like many others in the assisted living facility where she lived, she dreaded losing memory entirely, failing to recognize relatives and friends. I recall the heartbreaking morning when my colleague and friend, Don Murray, told me of his wife looking him in the face and asking, "Where's Don?" These sad transitions are the lot of all of us who watch the declining days and months of our parents.

We are caught in time, we experience our lives as a movement through time, and we tell stories to give shape and meaning to this passage. That is the human condition. Our understanding of history, science, our national identity, the very "selves" we have developed, rests on an accounting of time—"the stories of our lives become our lives."

The book you are about to read has no appearance of a conventional narrative. But at its core, there is a conflict between the ways we treat narrative in school (as a type of writing, often an easy one) and the central role narrative plays in our consciousness. The hero of this story is narrative itself—how it comes to our aid as we sort out the welter of information that is available, as it undergirds our belief that our world is comprehensible, and meaningful, and one in which our actions have consequences. Narrative is there to help us "compose" ourselves when we meet difficulty or loss. It is there to ground abstract ideas, to help us see the pattern in a set of numerical data, to illuminate the human consequences of political action. It is home base.

Narrative as a Type

Historically, the most common approach to sorting out types of writing has been the modes—description, narration, exposition, and argumentation. This has always been a problematical classification; James Kinneavy argued in his classic text, *A Theory of Discourse* (1971), that it confuses means and ends (e.g., exposition is an *end*, to inform; narration is a *means*). In tracing the history of the modes, Robert Connors (1999) has argued that they had a period of dominance but fell into disfavor, though in my view they are still alive and well, resurfacing in the Common Core State Standards (CCSS).

It was a short step from identifying these modes to making developmental claims about them. If we view reasoning as a late-blooming capacity, it follows that the natural progression is from description and narration (which rely on perception and memory) to exposition and argumentation (which rely more on generalization, analysis, and reasoning). So it makes sense to stress the less analytic modes in the lower grades and the more cognitively challenging modes in the upper grades; in fact, James Moffett, in his classic text, *Teaching the Universe of Discourse* (1968), makes that claim, as, implicitly, do the new CCSS, which mandate a move away from narrative toward argumentation in high school years. Two of the main authors of the literacy standards put it this way: "While narrative writing is given prominence in early grades, as students progress through the grades the Common Core State Standards increasingly ask students to write arguments or informational reports from sources" (Coleman and Pimental 2011, 11).

The CCSS create the triumvirate of narrative, informational, and argumentative writing—a clear instance of a "category error." A category error occurs when a classification is based on conflicting principles. Take, for example, Jose Louis Borges' fanciful classification of animals:

> On these pages it is written that animals are divided into (a) those that belong to the emperor, (b) embalmed ones, (c) those that are trained, (d) fabulous ones, (e) mermaids, (f) suckling pigs, (g) stray dogs, (h) those not included in this classification, (i) those that tremble as they are mad, (j) innumerable ones, (k) those drawn with a fine camel's hair brush, (l) others, (m) those that have not broken a vase, (n) those that resemble flies from a distance. (1953, 103)

"Fabulous ones" clearly would include "mermaids"; "stray dogs" would be included in "those that have not broken a vase." A category error would be to ask someone if they wanted dessert or ice cream. The answer could obviously be *both*.

In the case of the CCSS, there is a mixing of the aims of language use with modes of discourse, a confusion of ends and means. Narrative is a *form* or mode of discourse that can be used for multiple purposes (as I will show in this book)—we use it to inform, to persuade, to entertain, to express. It is the "mother of all modes," a powerful and innate form of understanding. "Informational writing and reading" refers to an aim or purpose of discourse. How, for example, would we classify Katherine Boo's Pulitzer Prize–winning account, *Behind the Beautiful Forevers* (2012)—narrative or informational? Clearly both. Argumentation would, in my view, be an element of persuasive writing, stripped of the ethos (focusing on the character of the speaker) and pathos (focusing on emotion). We will need narrative to accomplish the fuller rhetorical aim of persuasion.

Or how would we classify one of my favorite assignments? I invite students to pick some inanimate object that is in some way precious to them—best if it's the kind of thing no one else values. Then, address that object and provide details justifying that affection. So, are we talking argument or art? Narrative or persuasive? Here is my attempt that I share.

Fake Coals

A squat Weber Grill, black,
$29. Beginning to rust, of course
Left out in the rain, rarely cleaned
So that one day's marinate blends into the next.

My neighbor, with his $550 Weber extravaganza,
Must look on me with pity.
He's got temperature gauges, racks for meat, valves,
*   hood, wheels.*
A fat little propane tank with tubes to the grill.
Even temperature directions for cooking
I mean, if you need all that stuff, why not stay in
*   the house?*

"Isn't it slow," he must think. To have to wait for coals to
*   be ready.*
But if you are drinking Stella Artois (as you must when
*   you barbecue)*
What's wrong with slow?
Sometimes I look down at my coals and say
"Slow down kids, I'm liking this buzz."
I drink and wave to walkers in the neighborhood who
*   are totally*
Envious of me, inhaling the smoke clouds
Wafting from my Weber,
as they head home to tofu and salad.

Ok, so one day I had to borrow his behemoth because I had
*   a lot of people coming over*

I looked into the pit of his grill, where the fire jetted in
And I saw fake coals that would glow when lit.
Fake coals.

His big Weber was imitating my piece-of-shit grill.
Unsuccessfully.

The function of the piece is persuasive or literary, but it employs a set of small telescoped narratives and a fuller one to conclude. It makes no sense to see it as narrative or argumentative—it's both.

The CCSS challenge this dominance of fictional narratives and stress a movement toward complex analytic and expository texts—both in reading and writing—in the high school years. And at the elementary school level, they also stress a better balance of options. The predominance of narrative fiction, it is argued, does not prepare students for the college reading which, outside of English classes, is neither fictional nor narrative.

As someone who swims in the sea of argument and exposition, I fully support this broadening of opportunities. I remember my son's friend's asking me the rhetorical question: "Why should I read about something that didn't happen, when I can read about something that *did* happen?"

At the same time, there is a need to question the ways in which the lines are being drawn between "informational" reading and "narrative" reading. Reading researcher Nell Duke distinguishes the reading of informational texts in this way:

> *We typically read fictional narrative texts in their entirety, from beginning to end, at a steady pace. In contrast, we typically read informational texts selectively—just the parts that might meet our needs or interest us. We might start at the index, then check a passage on page 38, then read a whole section on page 15. We may vary the pace of reading from section to section, reading some parts carefully and just scanning others. (2004, 3)*

There is no question that this kind of piecemeal reading is part of what we all do. And many books and Internet resources are set up for just this kind of purpose. I will call this approach *extractive* reading—making forays into a text to find information for a purpose formed prior to the reading. I suspect most of our online reading is of this type; in fact, eye-tracking studies show that we view Internet pages in an F pattern, ignoring most of the page, and reading fewer than 20% of the words (National Dissemination Center for Children with Disabilities 2012). Jaime S. Fall, a nationally known human resources expert, has observed that young employees "are very good at finding information, but not as good at putting that information into context" (Tugend 2013).

These modes are also alive and well in discussions of comprehension—where the cognitive line between narration and exposition (or "informational texts") is clearly drawn. The following statement seems to me a consensus view of this distinction, and I will quote it at length:

> *Narrative texts contain artfully arranged sequences of events. Readers enter into the world the author has created or re-created and gain insight into the human condition. In contrast, readers don't expect things to "happen" in informational texts; they expect to acquire facts, learn opinions, obtain explanations, or find solutions to problems. Of course information can be presented in narrative form (e.g. biography) and a story may contain useful information, but readers do not ordinarily read narratives to obtain information, and they do not dip into informational texts to lose themselves in created worlds.*
>
> *The different purposes lead to different kinds of reading experiences. When following a narrative, the priority is the unfolding story; with exposition it is information. Thus the experience of reading a novel about a pioneer family is not the same as the experience of reading an article on the westward movement even though both are on the same topic.* (Hammond and Nessel 2012, 77)

This distinction tracks well the claim by Louise Rosenblatt that we approach expository texts with an "efferent" stance—to "carry away" information. By contrast, we approach literature with an "aesthetic" intent, to become immersed in the imagined world that is created for us. The verbs in the above quotation—"*obtain* information," "*acquire* facts"—are a clear indication of an *extractive* view of informational reading.

These authors make two claims that I will challenge in this book. First, that readers do not typically read narratives to get information—I will argue we do this all the time; in fact, we prefer to learn in this way. We normally don't take in information "raw." We seek out authors who can create explanatory patterns—as Rich Cohen does in this marvelous narrative paragraph his *National Geographic* piece on sugar.

*In school they call it the age of exploration, the search for territories
and islands that would send Europeans all around the world. In
reality it was, to no small degree, a hunt for fields where sugarcane
would prosper. In 1425 the Portuguese prince known as Henry the
Navigator sent sugarcane to Madeira with an early group of colo-
nists. The crop soon made its way to other newly discovered Atlantic
islands—the Cape Verde Islands, the Canaries. In 1493, when
Columbus set off on his second voyage to the New World, he too
carried cane. Thus dawned the age of big sugar, of Caribbean islands
and slave plantations, leading, in time, to great smoky refineries
on the outskirts of glass cities, to mass consumption, fat kids, obese
parents, and men in XXL tracksuits trundling along in electric carts.*
(2013, 86)

In 139 words Cohen is able to connect early Portuguese and Spanish exploration to overweight men in XXL tracksuits.

We like to learn American history through wonderful biographies, like
Doris Kearns Goodwin's *Team of Rivals* (2005) and David McCullough's
biography of John Adams (2001). Or for younger children books like
Cynthia Levinson's *We've Got a Job: The 1963 Birmingham Children's March*
(2012). In a later chapter we will look closely at how Denise Grady, science
writer for *The New York Times*, uses narrative to convey very technical
breakthroughs in medical research. Joy Hakim, author of an innovative
history series for students, puts it this way:

*It is through story that people have traditionally passed on their ideas,
their values, and their heritage. In recent years, however, we have
come to think of stories as the property of the youngest of our children.
How foolish of us. The rejection of story has made history seem dull.
It has turned it into a litany of facts and dates. Stories make the past
understandable (as well as enjoyable). Stories tell us who we are and
where we've been.* (2007, 4)

Obviously we all do much reading for extraction—to find a key fact or
quote, or follow up a teaser headline about some embarrassing statement made on *Dancing with the Stars*. We do this all the time. But if we do
extended reading of a complex topic or argument, we need writers to create
a *pattern*. And the most accessible pattern for human beings is some form
of narrative.

Take the book you are reading now. You *could* read this book piece-meal, skimming for my main idea, jumping to the end to see about any practical advice I can give. It's clearly your choice—literally in your hands. But as a writer I will work to *keep you with me,* to follow the turns of thought and evidence—and to do this I need to develop patterns that I will call a "plot." I want to create that sense that we will "transgress" together, think the unthinkable—as we challenge established views of how we read and write nonfiction.

A second claim is that with narrative texts we "enter into the world of the author" but that with informational texts we do not—primarily because nothing "happens" in these texts. We stay more outside of them; we use them, but we don't enter them. This too seems a debatable asser-tion. Take Stephen Ambrose's *Undaunted Courage: Meriwether Lewis, Thomas Jefferson, and the Opening of the American West* (1996), which I read recently. To be sure, I learned a lot about this amazing expedition and a fair amount of U.S. geography; but I was also totally immersed in the story, as much as if I were reading a novel. The heartbreaking conclusion, with Meriwether Lewis losing his mind and committing suicide, is as poignant as any scene in a novel. In other words, Ambrose's narrative skill helped me hold on to information, but my experience of reading was also emotional, aesthetic, fully entering the "world" he created for me.

One way to deal with this issue is to claim that there is of course "overlap"—that informational texts often contain *some* narrative, a sort of minor ingredient. But I will argue that the problem is more than some messy overlap. Even scientific discourse, normally thought so distant from narrative, depends on establishing causal relationships or sequences, even stories. Photosynthesis is a story; climate change is a story; cancer is a story, with antecedents and consequences. To the extent these phenomena can be *told* as stories, readers will have a better chance of taking in the informa-tion. (I'll put a little foundation under that claim in the next chapter.) And in fact, the CCSS recognize the ways in which we mix types of writing:

> Students' narrative skills continue to grow in these grades. The Standards require that students be able to incorporate narrative elements effectively into arguments and informative/explanatory texts. In history/social studies, students must be able to incorporate narrative accounts into their analyses of individuals or events of historical import. (National Governors Association Center for Best Practices and Council of Chief State School Officers 2010a)

Although this is a step in the right direction, I will argue for a more prominent function for narrative, as something more than an "element" in other types of writing.

It also seems to me that if we look—honestly—at how we *prefer to* learn information, we seek out writers who can embed it in narrative. When I read the best analytic writing—the work of Pollan, Gladwell, Gould, Lehrer, Kolbert, my favorite columnists—it often *feels* like a story to me. The writing unfolds. I enjoy the playing out of ideas and positions, the ways they conflict, the ways in which questions are raised and explored—the way they are narrated. All of these writers are masters of the embedded story that grounds any point in live experience, which gives it what rhetoricians call *presence*. A news article on a cancer breakthrough will employ a *case*, a patient's story, to help us understand the science. This work confirms the claim of Robert Frost that "everything written is as good as it is dramatic. It need not declare itself in form, but it is drama or it is nothing" (in Poirier 1997, 452).

Louise Rosenblatt, the great proponent of transactional reading, attempted to deal with this question by claiming there was a "spectrum" or range of texts between efferent texts (where the purpose was conveying information) and aesthetic texts (where the purpose is immersion in a created world). On a spectrum, to move in one direction, you move away from another; that's the way a spectrum works.

But is that the way reading works? Does Emerson, for example, become less aesthetic by trying to convey propositions? Are we dealing with a zero-sum game, more of one thing means less of another? Or could we imagine that writing could become more effectively informative by employing the aesthetic features of plot, characterization, and narration? In other words, the communication of information could be enhanced (and made more pleasurable for the reader) by the skillful employment of forms we might call *literary*. I will argue that there is solid cognitive research to support this view.

Take an example from my own reading history—Roy Chapman Andrews' *All About Dinosaurs* (1953), which I read in late elementary school. It was clearly an informational book, but one that mesmerized young readers with Andrews' accounts of his field work in the Gobi Desert. I absolutely loved the dinosaur names, like Iguanodon, or Triceratops, or Seismosaurus, a plant eater half as long as a football field, that (we suspect) shook the earth when it walked. It was thrilling to read about the discovery of fossilized dinosaur eggs. I still recall a decision his team made to use the little flour they had left for research rather than for food. The gratification that I gained was both aesthetic and efferent. It came from an immersion in the narrative *and* the information of dinosaurs. There was a romance to this information. I had the best of both worlds.

words

The extractive model for reading fails to account for the ways we accomplish *sustained* acts of reading. To sustain a reading, a reader must sense a pattern, what I will call a "plot." In other words, "purpose" is not entirely something that the reader brings to the text—but an orientation that the *writer* helps the reader form. We struggle when writers fail to do this well. The great rhetorical Kenneth Burke called literary form "an arousing and fulfillment of desires" (1968, 124), clearly the sexiest definition of form I know of. And I will extend that to all sustained reading. We don't read extended texts through sheer grit, but we are carried along by some pattern the writer creates. Even if our goal is to learn information, we don't do that well if that information is not connected in some way—and as humans the connection we crave is narrative.

I will use the terms *plot* and *story* in an expansive way to describe how we read texts that we would not normally think of as narrative in any way. My work draws on a central observation that Peter Elbow makes in his award-winning essay, "The Shifting Relationships Between Speech and Writing" (2000). He begins with the obvious point that in sustained reading we process words "in time." We can't take in the whole text at once, spatially, as we might a picture or building. *Structure* only has meaning, human efficacy, if it holds together the temporal moments of our reading. How, then, do we accomplish this?

Elbow wrestles with this question of how we sustain a reading and resolves the problem this way—if there is a text for the sermon of this book, here it is:

> Thus, the problem of structure in a temporal medium is really the
> problem of how to bind time. Whereas symmetry and pattern bind
> space (and also bind smaller units of time—in the form of rhythm),

they don't manage very well to hold larger units of time together.
What binds larger units of time? Usually it is the experience of
anticipation or tension which then builds to some resolution or
satisfaction. In well-structured discourse, music, and films (temporal
media) we almost invariably see a pattern of alternating dissonance—
and—consonance or itch and then scratch. Narrative is probably the
most common and natural way to set up a structure of anticipation
and resolution in discourse. (2000, 163)

The implications of Elbow's claim are, in my view, profound—and this book might be viewed as an attempt to work out what it means for the reading and writing of expository and argumentative texts.

He asks us to rethink what we mean by *form* or *structure*. As often presented to students, structure (the outline for example) is static, a set of claims and supports. It is spatial, architectural, and silent about the motives for the reader. As Elbow describes form, it is dynamic, seductive, active, and operating in time; it is a form of energy that the writing generates to sustain reading.

The practical question for teaching, then, is how can we teach students to attune themselves to texts, to align themselves with this generative energy? And as a mirror, the task of the writer is how to invite and guide this kind of mutual involvement? Put another way, how can a writer convince a reader to "stay with me"—and not to skip and sample? These are questions this book will address.

Another implication of Elbow's claim is that we read well-structured nonfiction in the same way we read fiction—and that "understanding" is not the absolute or only goal. Another heretical notion. It is a truism, a circular and almost unquestioned belief, that we read informational writing for . . . , well, information. It is the functional antithesis to literary reading. It is the sober, rational, practical, and duller older brother. We build our store of knowledge with it. The very term *comprehension* has as a root the concept of "holding" or "containing"—and seems to fit an extractive view of reading. Missing from this perspective is the sense of reading as an "experience," an undergoing, a patterned movement through time—and by extension a source of pleasure and satisfaction.

My own reading of excellent nonfiction doesn't work in this extractive way. Take for example *The Emperor of All Maladies: A Biography of Cancer* (Mukherjee 2010), winner of the 2011 Pulitzer Prize, and arguably one of the greatest pieces of expository writing in the last decade. If anyone were to give me a quiz on the information in this book—ask me to name the major experimenters or even to give a rudimentary account of the cell biology work described in the latter part of the book, I would fail miserably. And who knows how much I will retain a year from now? Yet reading this book was one of my most thrilling and gratifying experiences in years.

What did I get, if not information?

What I got was the *experience* of being with the author as he led me through the cycles of hope and defeat, through the carnage of so many patients in such grueling trials, and the hesitant but steady progress of researchers. I retain the sensation of "cancer" itself becoming the main character of the book—evasive, adaptive, persistent, multiple, an adversary of extraordinary wiliness and devastation. I retain these narrative contours—and the information I retain adheres to them (e.g., the role of Sidney Farber, who believed that childhood leukemia could be treated).

The great value of works like this, like good fiction, is that we put ourselves in the hands of someone else. Wayne Booth put it this way:

> *The author makes his readers. If he makes them badly—that is, if he simply waits, in all purity, for the occasional reader whose perceptions and norms happen to match his own, then his conception must be lofty indeed if we are to forgive him for his bad craftsmanship. But if he makes them well—that is he makes them see what they have never seen before, moves them into a new order of perception and experience altogether—he finds his reward in the peers he has created. (1961, 397–98)*

We sign on for the journey.

If we only read for bits of information, if all nonfiction is viewed as a glorified phone book, we simply plug that information into preexisting schema and we don't change (which is why I think a lot of Internet reading only confirms prejudices). Wikipedia would suffice. For only by moving outside ourselves, by opening ourselves to difference, can we have any hope of being changed, of being educated (literally being "led out"). As William James reminds us, "in the matter of belief we are all extreme conservatives" (1954, 172); we struggle to maintain the status quo, to stay as we are. Our best chance to grow, perhaps our only chance, is to travel.

To be taken into a book like *The Emperor of All Maladies* is to move outside ourselves and to be present as a first-rate mind explains the science and human drama of cancer research. It is to experience another sensibility, to sense how the writer notices, contemplates, values. I suspect this fellow-traveling is the great lasting benefit we get from sustained reading of good nonfiction, one that seeps into our writing—or so we hope.

No More Hamburgers

This problem of sustained reading is mirrored in writing instruction. To write, at least to write seriously, is to imagine a reading act, to convince the reader "I am with you and know how it is." But in so many classrooms, rigid formulaic structures prevail. How we voluntarily read—and how students are taught to write—could hardly be farther apart. Formula does not equal form—one is static, the other dynamic.

I was taught the "school essay" in the mid-1960s. I keenly recall my own introduction to the five-paragraph model; we were given a diagram of this essay with three rectangular "body" paragraphs, contained by two facing triangles, one for the opening paragraph and one for the conclusion. We were told to start generally and move to the thesis at the end of the first paragraph, make a point and defend it in each of the body paragraphs, and then conclude by reversing the pattern of the opening and move from the specific thesis to a broader statement. These opening and closing triangles were actually fairly hard to write, so the directions were simplified to the basic "say what you are going to say/say it/then say what you said."

I have since heard this model referred to as the "hamburger" format with the opening and closing paragraphs being the two buns and the body being the meat. This has always seemed to me not only a disservice to students, and to nonfiction writing, but also an insult to hamburgers— because they, after all, have more variety than that (double-cheese, bacon burger, pretzel burgers, even burgers with fries in the bun).

I have tried to trace the origins of this formula, and the closest I can come is Lucile Vaughn Payne's very popular writing text, *The Lively Art of Writing*, first published in 1965, where I have located the diagram. (And to be fair she never states that five paragraphs is a fixed goal.) The dates work out, though my eleventh-grade teacher would have had to be quick on the uptake to get it to us so soon after publication. But it may have had an even earlier start, for when Janet Emig published her classic case study in 1971, the five-paragraph theme was endemic, "indigenously American," as if written to the accompaniment "Kate Smith singing 'God Bless America' or the piccolo obligato from 'The Stars and Stripes Forever'" (93). Like many subsequent critics, she finds the form redundant and utterly divorced from the popular writing of the time.

Since Emig's classic jab, the five-paragraph theme has been a whipping boy because it is so controlled by a thesis and it provides little space, or incentive, for exploration. David Bartholomae makes this criticism:

> If . . . we ask students to write about texts, the tyranny of the thesis often invalidates the very act of analysis we hope to invoke. Hence, in assignment after assignment, we find students asked to reduce a novel, a poem, or their own experience into a single sentence, and then to use the act of writing in order to defend or "support" that single sentence. Writing is used to close a subject down rather than open it up, to put an end to discourse rather than open up a project. (1983, 311)

Peter Elbow has called it an "anti-perplexity machine" (2012, 309) because there is no room for the untidiness of inquiry or complexity.

In the many arguments I have had on the five-paragraph theme, I regularly hear the defense that students need to learn the form first, and then it can be modified and made more complex later on. I suspect this development occurs for many writers, but this argument has always seemed to me suspect, even dangerous, as it can cover many sins. Teach them an inauthentic form, and later on they can learn the real one ("You'll need this later"). These inauthentic forms have the virtue of simplicity, and seem more teachable. But when we strip human motives from our teaching, I suspect that we make learning harder and not easier. In this book, I will try to show this more dynamic approach to exposition and argument.

Nonfiction, I will argue, is all about *moves*, motion through time. Not static structures. The key feature what Kenneth Burke calls "symbolic action" (1966). If all works well, we are carried forward as we read, sustained, even dare I say *seduced* by the writer who may, herself, have felt this motion in the act of writing as the topic seemed to open up, as she "listened to the text," which at times seemed to take on a life of its own.

So my claim is this: that in representation of reading and writing nonfiction, we have generally failed to account for how the process really works when we are engaged. In the area of reading, we have labored under "extractive" models that fail to account for sustained attention; we have acted as if the goal is simply to get "information" and not to be fully committed to the nonfiction text.

A BAKER'S DOZEN OF SELF-PROMPTS OR **HOW WE GIVE OURSELVES A CONFERENCE**

1. What happens next?
2. What does it look like, feel like, smell like?
3. How can I restate that?
4. What's my reaction to that?
5. What example or experience can I call up to illustrate that?
6. What's my evidence?
7. What parts of my prior reading can I bring to bear on that?
8. What comparison can I make that makes that clearer?
9. Why does that matter?
10. What do I mean by that?
11. Who else would agree with that? Disagree? What would they say?
12. How can I qualify that statement? What are the exceptions?
13. How does that fit into larger debates or controversies?

In the teaching of writing, we have labored under formulaic models that have the same problem—they fail to provide guidance in how writers maintain the loyal attention of readers. We have presented form as a visual structure, not as a series of "moves." Because I am asking you (are you still there?) to keep with me for the next 150 pages, this is a very real issue. Like Walt Whitman I want you to believe that "I am with you and know how it is."

But there are resources for sustained reading, and the very best, the most gratifying, the most comprehensible, the most familiar one is narrative. But we will have to think about it in a new way, not in the traditional way as a mode (an *easy one*) alongside other modes. We will have to make a mess of all that.

There is then a weaker and a stronger claim for the centrality of narrative. The weaker claim is that even in writing that is predominantly analytic or expository, writers need to ground their claims with examples or instances—told as stories. (John Dewey and Ralph Waldo Emerson are so difficult to read because they refused to do this!) The CCSS even acknowledge this, though only in an appendix. This claim is, in my view, self-evidently true; it hardly needs support. Locate any widely read writer on science or medicine or the environment and you will find someone skilled at narrative writing, one who keeps before our eyes the human consequences of policies and discoveries. One reason that so-called "academic" writers are held in low esteem by the wider public is their resistance to employing narrative—cutting them off from a wider readership.

But there is a strong version of this argument that will need some work. In fact, it goes so much against the grain that you may want to take it as simply a thought experiment, a kind of "what if?"

So here is my modest proposition. That narrative is the deep structure of all good sustained writing. *All good writing.* We struggle with writers who dispense with narrative form and simply present information (a major problem with some textbooks)—because we are given no frame for comprehension. Mark Turner, a cognitive psychologist and literary critic, puts the claim this way: "Narrative imagining—story—is the fundamental instrument of thought. Rational capacities depend on it. It is our chief means of looking into the future, of predicting, of planning, of explaining" (1996, 4–5; see also Eubanks 2004). My former colleague Donald Murray made the claim this way:

> We study all the variations of narrative in short story, novel, stage, screen, and television drama, but rarely examine the narrative that is embedded in all effective writing—the proposal for a new marketing plan, the essay on health care, the insurance investigators report, the sermon, the scholarship application, the restraining order, the memorial service remarks. All are built on the sturdy and time-tested foundation of narrative.
>
> If we are to become successful writers and rewriters we must develop the craft to create and hide the narrative that underlies most effective writing. The reader does not need to see the intestines of the writer, but the narrative and the human organs must be in place and working. (2004, 89–90)

"Create and hide." A fascinating observation. Even writing that takes a form we would not call narrative (e.g., the lab report) still is built on narrative, on a causal understanding of the world that is as basic to us as, well, our intestines. This claim is true for even the most specialized academic writing; even research reports must tell a story.

I will argue that we have much to gain from this perspective:

- It identifies a broad unifying principle.
- It can help students bridge from more familiar to less familiar genres of writing. That is, even when students approach a new situation or discipline, there will be common features and familiar strategies to help manage new reading and writing tasks.
- It challenges the reductive writing approaches that mistakenly counsel students to get their thesis set early in an essay, before there is even a *need* for a thesis, some conflict or tension that needs resolving.
- It is consistent with the cycle of human thought—which as John Dewey argues is an "experience" of working through a problem to a resolution, however provisional; or as Jean Piaget claimed, a movement from disequilibrium to an integration and accommodation of new information. It tracks the movement of mind, creates a narrative of our thinking.
- It accounts for the artistry of excellent expository and argumentative writing: the ways in which writers set up tensions and problems, the ways they employ cases, and the ways they put multiple voices and positions in conflict—in sum, the ways in which they dramatize thinking and discovery. In doing so, they not only enhance our ability to take in information—they create a sense of pleasure in doing so.
- It calls the bluff on much textbook writing—which regularly *fails* to provide a satisfactory pattern for comprehension. (We will look at some examples in Chapter 4.)
- It accounts more successfully for the motivation to read. Writers need to elicit and sustain a *desire* to read on.

We have been habituated to see the types of writing we name as truly distinct. We are always tempted to believe that names correspond to distinct entities—that narration and exposition are different forms of discourse created and understood by distinct cognitive processes. In other words, we can be seduced by our own linguistic labels.

So, it may help to abandon them, at least for the space of this book, and to entertain the claim that there is a deep and teachable structure to all sustained writing—one that gratifies our fundamental need for plot, for the establishment of tension and resolution, for a pattern to motivate and sustain reading, and for a *teller*, some guide to take us through.

MINDS MADE FOR STORIES

Action is eloquence.

WILLIAM SHAKESPEARE, *CORIOLANUS*

In the now-forgotten 1970s movie, *Lovers and Other Strangers*, Richard Castellano (later of *Godfather* fame) plays the working class Catholic father of Mike, who is about to marry into a Waspish upper-class family. The movie is a sex farce—swirling around him are an impending divorce of his other son, various affairs, troubled marriages, the near-decision of his son to call the whole thing off, memories of an earlier love, Mary Rose, and his own less than ideal marriage. As he tries to sort things out, he continually asks, "What's the story?"

He is not asking to be entertained with a narrative; he wants an explanation. He wants to understand causes; why is this chaos occurring all around him? He wants some sense of cause and effect—and he uses the term *story* to describe the understanding he hopes to gain.

It is this sense of "story" that I want to explore in this chapter. By this point I have made some fairly grandiose claims about narrative and comprehension without troubling to provide much evidence or psychological underpinning. And this evidence exists in abundance. The place of causality in comprehension, indeed human understanding, has been intensively studied. In fact, our predisposition to experience reality as story, as cause-effect, is now viewed as innate as language itself. We are always asking, "What's the story?"

In his fascinating book, *Thinking, Fast and Slow*, Daniel Kahneman illustrates this longing for causation. He begins with our reaction to a simple pair of words he asks us to read:

> *Bananas*   *Vomit*

> *A lot happened to you during the last second or two. You experienced some unpleasant images and memories. Your face twisted slightly in an expression of disgust, and you may have pushed the book imperceptibly farther away. Your heart rate increased, the hair on your arms rose a little, and your sweat glands were activated. In short you responded with an attenuated version of how you would react to the actual event. All of this was completely automatic, beyond your control.* (2011, 50)

His use of the word *event* is significant because we have not been given an event, only two words. But we make it into an event (someone eating a banana and subsequently throwing up as a result) through the use an automatic form of processing that Kahneman calls System 1 or "fast" thinking:

> *In a second or so you accomplished, automatically and unconsciously, a remarkable feat. Starting from a completely unexpected event, your System 1 made as much sense as possible—two simple words, oddly juxtaposed—by linking the words in a causal story.* (2011, 52)

As he uses the word *story* (and as I will), it is not a literary form, but an embodied and instinctive mode of understanding.

As another example we can take the *Sports Illustrated* jinx, known to anyone who has ever subscribed or looked beyond the swimsuit issue. It goes like this. It's late June and a relatively unknown center fielder is hitting over .400. This is a magic number, because no one has batted .400 in a season since Ted Williams did it in 1941. This young phenom's photo appears on the cover with a caption: "Will this be the year?" You can probably guess the rest: the hitter goes into a slump, his average descends to closer to his regular, lifetime .270 average.

If you believe in the jinx (as I do), you read the situation as cause and effect. Getting your picture on the cover of *SI* causes the decline. This jinx, in a way I can't articulate, affects the psychology of the batter (makes him too self-conscious, too confident) and undermines the hot streak. Anyone who has seen a local star on the cover says a quiet "Oh, shit" as they wait for inevitable (and dare I say unnecessary) collapse.

Of course, I know better.

There is a far more plausible, but less interesting and gratifying, explanation. The law of averages just catches up with this hitter. His average reverts to closer to his base level of performance; he may have a better year than average, but he is no Ted Williams. We can see this same tendency in the recent effort by the Gates Foundation to advocate for smaller high schools, since the best performing schools were small. We instinctively read cause and effect into that fact—there is something about smallness, the intimacy of teachers and students, for example, that makes smallness a cause of higher performance.

But statistically, you would expect this to be the case; you'd also expect the worst schools to be small as well (which is also true). With fewer teachers, it would be more likely to get a cluster of excellent ones in a school; but the odds would also be better that you'd get a cluster of poor teachers in the same school. Larger schools would regress toward a mean, as they would inevitably have a mix of teaching ability. It was an appealing plausible story, just not true.

It is difficult to overstate the role of causation in our understanding of the world—and by extension our comprehension of texts. We are biologically predisposed to process experience through the lens of antecedents and consequences; it explains graduation speeches, the way we experience tragedy ("Everything happens for a reason"), the "stories" of political candidates, the enduring place of religion, the resistance to theories of evolution (and to statistics), superstitions *and* the scientific theories that overturned them, even the way we prefer active sentences in our reading. We perceive all human encounters as forms of intentional action (we *read* people)—we are called on to react in some way. The inability to read intentions is a devastating disability. According to Kahneman, "The perception of intention and emotion is irresistible; only people with autism do not experience it" (2011, 76).

Although causality has always been seen as central to human understanding, it was traditionally conceived as something *learned* from experience, a claim made by the philosopher David Hume. We see a number of cases where B follows A and we generalize that experiences like A cause those like B. But Immanuel Kant challenged this view, claiming that humans innately view experience in terms of causality; we are hardwired to do so—very likely a useful evolutionary adaptation. He essentially reversed Hume's claim that causal understanding was "derived" from experience—

rather "experience" itself is derived from our predisposition to see things in a causal way (De Pierris and Friedman 2013).

A set of experiments by the Belgian psychologist Albert Michotte (1963) demonstrated that even infants are primed to perceive causality. He would have them watch a black square, projected on a screen, that moves toward a red square, comes in contact with it, and the red square begins to move away. The perception, irresistibly, is that the red square is "launched" by the black square, and infants are surprised when this doesn't happen. In other words, Michotte and subsequent researchers demonstrated that causality was not something learned, inductively, from experience—it is something we see, in the same way we see color. It is not something derived from experience; it is the way we construct experience in the first place.

As I write, the country is in deep mourning for children and adults massacred in Newtown, Connecticut. We collectively cling to details and try to piece together a narrative that might begin to explain how any human could turn a high-powered assault weapon on young children. Was mental illness of some kind a cause? What do we make of the fact that his mother was a teacher—is that relevant? And the fact that he used her guns—and she, herself was a victim? Where was the father in all this? Can any of this help explain the tragedy (and even to call it a *tragedy* is evidence of our desire for a coherent story). We try for this coherence because incoherence is terrifying. We need stories, not simply for some aesthetic pleasure, but to reassure ourselves that we live in a comprehensible world. As Joan Didion writes:

> We tell ourselves stories in order to live. We look for the sermon in the suicide, the social or moral lesson in the murder of five. We interpret what we see, select the most workable of multiple choices. We live entirely, especially if we are writers, by the imposition of a narrative line upon disparate images, by the "ideas" with which we have learned to freeze the shifting phantasmagoria, which is our actual experience. (1979, 11)

Yes, But . . .

Whenever I make this broad claim for narrative or story I run into a problem with terminology. The term *story* is so embedded as a genre or type of writing that the reimagining I am proposing runs into rough headwinds.

Mark Turner makes the same observation in his compelling book, *The Literary Mind*: "Written works called narratives or stories may be shelved in a special section of the bookstore, but the mental instrument that I call narrative or story is basic to human thinking" (1996, 7). It might be argued that "causality" and "story" or "narrative" are really not as identical as I make them out to be (though, as we have seen previously, Kahneman and Turner clearly link them).

Some would make the distinction that narrative or story is about a specific event in time and place, where informational texts deal with that which is *generally* true. James Moffett (1968) makes a distinction between narrative (what happened) and expository writing (what happens). I would argue though that even when we are talking about "what happens," we make use of the tools of narration (characters, plot, conflict), as in this account of corn sex, written by Elizabeth Kolbert:

> Corn's female organs are sheathed in a sort of vegetable chastity belt—surrounded by a tough, virtually impenetrable husk. The only way in is by means of a silk thread that each flower extends, Rapunzel-like, through a small opening. For fertilization to take place, a grain of pollen must land on the tip of the silk, then shimmy its way six to eight inches through a microscopic tube, a journey that requires several hours. The result of a successful passage is a single kernel. (2012, 19)

Kolbert writes a narrative of this process, with the heroic bit of pollen, and even invokes a fairy tale to help us understand the sequence of events.

There is also the practical problem that my focus on story will be taken to mean that all we need to do is to teach students about stories—and they will automatically be able to operate in all genres (obviously not true). In my first book, *More than Stories*, I tried to make the case for a repertoire of reading and writing opportunities, and I still believe that. Or that this argument could be taken as an effort to stop the invasion of informational texts in schools (also not true). I love nonfiction (after all, I'm writing it now!)—but I also want to understand how it really works in extended reading, how it invites us the stay with a writer, and how, when it really works, it draws on innate predispositions and capacities for understanding.

After one of these readers-will-misinterpret-you conversations, I began to sketch out on an envelope a sort of triangle that may help explain my redefinition. The model I am proposing has four levels, with the bottom level representing innate capacities and predispositions—instinctive, biological, foundational, innate (see Figure 2.1). The great sociologist Emile Durkheim put it this way:

> At the source of our judgements are a certain number of essential notions that dominate our entire intellectual life. These are what philosophers since Aristotle have called the categories of understanding: notions of time, space, genus, number, cause, personality, and so on. They correspond to the most universal properties of things. They are the solid frames that enclose thought. (2001, 11)

These "notions" are broadly *human* ways of understanding and experiencing the world.

It is at this level that we have Kahneman's System 1 thinking, our causal "thinking" as we reacted to the banana–vomit pairing. I place "causality" at this level, and because narrative is the primary way we express causality, I am claiming it is part of our deep structure as human beings.

As we move up the triangle, we progress to more learned and socially specific uses of language. The aims of discourse describe the broad

**Level 4
—Usage**
Any specific, particularized use of language (i.e., this book)

Level 3—Genres
The many socially specific ways in which we use language to accomplish the aims in Level 2—office memo, short story, tweet, scientific paper, etc. (Barwashi)

Level 2—Aims of Discourse
The social purposes for which we use language—identified by James Kinneavy as referential (informative), persuasive, literary, and expressive. Each focuses on a feature of the rhetorical triangle (subject, audience, language, and speaker).

Level 1—Innate Capacities
Universal and innate predispositions, fears, desires, and modes of expression and understanding—to include syntax, space, resemblance, causality. Kahneman's System 1 thinking would be at this level. They are instinctual, hard-wired, the product of long evolutionary development, foundational.

Figure 2.1 A Model for Story as the Structure of Thinking and Understanding

purposes for which we use language; I believe we could also place at this level broadly applicable rhetorical principles like the use of ethical, logical, and emotional appeals. Moving up the scale, genres specify the ways we achieve these aims and the myriad social situations we participate in (and they change with technology), culminating in an individual instance of an utterance or piece of writing—the top of the triangle.

No one level predetermines the level above it, but it constrains or forms the foundation for use at that level. The uses of language (level 2) are built on our innate need for society, for being in community (level 1). Genres (level 3) are methods for achieving human aims for language use (i.e., the memo is one form of persuasion, and there are an infinite range of memo subgenres). Any individual act of language use is guided, often unconsciously, by learned patterns of cultural discourse, our sense, for example of what a fable or job interview is. These shape that act of writing, without determining it. In fact, most of the sentences in this book have never been written before.

So back to the confusion about terminology: I believe the disagreement is about my placing story at such a deep level. The more conventional way, as I note in Chapter 1, is to treat it simply as a "mode of discourse" or as a genre (i.e., level 3), with many variants (anecdote, case study, short story). But if we view it as a deep structure of thinking and understanding, it affects all discourse and plays a much bigger role; we have literary minds, primed for story.

It also resolves the conflict about teaching—yes, we need to teach students the conventions of various genres, and we can't assume that because they can read and write fictional stories or autobiographical pieces that they can write arguments or reports. Only a magician could think that. But it does mean that the narrative thread, the anecdote, the story of human interest, the apt metaphor are crucial tools in all forms of discourse—as they speak to our need for causality and story. They form a deep structure.

Becoming Heroes of Our Own Stories

Constructing causal narratives also allows us to imagine ourselves as agents, even heroes, in our own life stories, which can be purposeful and coherent ("things happen for a reason"). Psychologist Shelley Taylor summarizes a range of studies to argue that this heroic representation of self, although not fully realistic, has major positive benefits for personal happiness. This exaggerated sense of personal agency emerges so power-fully and quickly in early childhood that it is very likely "natural [and] intrinsic to the cognitive system"(1989, 44). Like the evolution of organs or immune systems, it may be hardwired to support the perpetuation of the species—as anthropologist Lionel Tiger (his real name) has argued "optimism is a biological phenomenon" (1979, 40). The key beneficial illusion is a heightened sense of being able to master one's environment by acting in a causal way:

> *The illusion of control, a vital part of people's beliefs about their attributes, is a personal statement about how positive outcomes will be achieved, not merely by wishing and hoping that they will happen, but by making them happen through one's own capabilities.* (41)

Of course, events are not in our complete control, and humans face trauma and tragedy. Luck and chance play a huge role in any life. But even victims of terrible illness and loss are often able to derive meaning and benefit from their situation, perhaps working to inform or help others in their same situation.

Taylor's argument is supported by a line of research on "explanatory style" conducted by Martin Seligman (1991). *Explanatory style* refers to the ways in which individuals account for the difficulties they face; for example, whether they see themselves as victims or agents, whether they see diffi-culties arising from a pervasive character flaw ("I'm just not good at math") or a poor one-time decision that can be instructive in future situations ("I need to start preparing for the test earlier"). In doing so, they build a narra-tive of recovery, redemption, resilience.

Seligman's research demonstrates that when individuals fail to view themselves as agents in their lives, when they experience "learned helplessness," the consequences—for physical and mental health—are profound. In addition to a long-standing association with depression, researchers now believe that this explanatory style is an ineffective way of dealing with stress; it can compromise the immune system, leaving the individual susceptible to a range of infectious diseases. Not surprisingly, a "healthy" explanatory style is associated with increased motivation, persis-tence, and educational achievement. How we tell our stories matters.

This work on explanatory styles has given me a new appreciation for the stories students tell of their own development, particularly their capacity to transform the difficulties they face into constructive challenges. Take this application essay from Veneicia, a student in a program to prepare minority, first-generation students to apply to college. She begins by distinguishing "lucky" kids, those with stable lives and numerous opportunities, with "thankful" ones like her, dependent on a single parent living in poverty.

> *I grew up not knowing who my father was. He was never around and probably never even knew I existed. My mom struggled with the rent and expenses for me. Sometimes we didn't have to worry about rent because we were homeless. But then, somehow, my mom managed to pull it off and get us shelter. "I never asked to be in this situation so why is this happening to me?" That is the question I would continually ask myself. Why did my life have to be so difficult and different from other people. I used to think God was punishing me for a mistake I made in a previous life. But later in life, as I started growing and maturing, I realized that it was all just a test to see if I could face a challenge without giving up. And I passed. I used to think I was a "thankful" child, but now I realize that I am a lucky child. I have made it through life with only one parent. Yes, it was hard. But I did it with my mother as my inspiration.* (Early and DeCosta 2012, 91)

In Veneicia's essay, she shows the shift between the two explanatory styles that Seligman describes. At first she is passive—"Why is this happening to me?" But, with her mother as an example, she shifts to viewing her difficulties as a "test," and she has the resources and model to help her face challenges. By analogizing to the "passing a test" frame, she has constructed a narrative of agency. Paul Tough, in his book, *How Children Succeed: Grit, Curiosity, and the Hidden Power of Character* (2012), echoes Seligman's claim that this form of self-understanding, this self-narrative, is crucial for academic success.

There is now research to suggest that telling family stories and knowing family histories can also create a collective sense of resilience and stability. Psychologist Robyn Fivush (2011) and her colleagues developed a measure called "Do You Know?" which asked children questions like: Do you know where your parents met? Do you know the story of your birth? Do you know where your parents went to high school? It turned out that those children who knew this family history had a stronger sense of control of their own lives, higher self-esteem, and a belief that their families functioned effectively (Feiler 2013). Fivush and other researchers found that one type of story, the oscillating family narrative ("We've had our ups and downs as a family"), is especially important in shaping a healthy "intergenerational self." Even the military has begun to use the history of fighting units to create cohesion and camaraderie, for example, taking recruits to cemeteries—as have companies who use their histories to create employee and consumer loyalty.

Which brings me to the role of Rico Carty in the Newkirk family. In my final year at Oberlin College, I invited a few of my friends to come to my house in Ashland, just an hour away. My three male friends got into an argument about baseball, about who was leading the major league in batting (that's what guys do, right?). It went back and forth, Carl Yastrzemski, Tony Oliva, maybe Pete Rose. Then the one female in the group, Beth Gerngross, said, "It's Rico Carty." As might be expected, we dismissed her suggestion on the solid prejudice of gender—how could a woman know this? But she insisted that we check the *Cleveland Plain Dealer* to resolve the debate.

And she was right.

In fact, Carty would go on to win the National League batting championship with an average of .366, a great year. This stompdown by a woman, on baseball statistics, caused me to pay attention to her. I liked her boldness, the fact that she paid attention to sports (and she was very cute). We ended up married, and are married to this day, enjoying this fall the Red Sox great postseason. And as our kids came along, we would tell them the Rico Carty story, with some embellishments. "If it wasn't for Rico Carty, we would never have gotten married. You kids wouldn't even exist. We owe it all to him." (Talk about causality!) He became an oddly significant figure in our family history.

For our twenty-fifth wedding anniversary, the story came full circle. Our older daughter contacted the Cleveland Indians, where Carty had finished his career as a base coach, and they agreed to forward an anniversary card to him in Puerto Rico. He signed it and returned it to us, with a lovely message in his non-native language, wishing us "a very Brite future and Happiness."

"I Write Subject-Verb-Object Sentences"

This affection for causality can even be seen at the sentence level. My former colleague, National Book Award winner Tom Williams, was once asked what he wrote. And he answered, "I write subject-verb-object sentences." These sentences satisfy our desire for action and consequences;

they make for clarity and vigor in writing. As Joseph Williams writes in his classic book, *Style: Ten Lessons in Clarity and Grace*:

> *A clear and direct style depends first on how we express action. As we'll use the word here, action will cover many notions: movement, feeling, process, change, activity, condition—physical or mental, literal or figurative. The important point is this: While we cannot always express action in a verb, in the clearest and most vigorous sentences, we usually do.* (1981, 9–10)

Writers regularly drain any vigor from their writing by obscuring this action: through using passive sentences, keeping the reader from the action, or framing the action in a noun rather than a verb ("we completed a review" versus "we reviewed"). The most comprehensible sentences take a dramatic form; a subject acting upon an object. Bureaucratic language is hard to read because this action, dare I say this narrative, is obscured.

As we will see in Chapter 4, textbooks frequently fail to exploit this need for direct action—and in doing so create problems for readers. This need for action in sentences is as true for writing we call narrative as it is for other forms of writing. Even more theoretical writing works best when there is *cognitive energy*—the sense of an active mind at work.

Causality and Comprehension

Cognitive researchers have exhaustively studied the role of causality in the understanding of narrative texts. This marriage is not surprising since "plot" is all about causality. As E. M. Forster famously wrote: "The king died and the queen died of grief is a plot" (1956, 86). Plots exploit our natural predilection to see events ordered in chronological sequences that show antecedents (the king died) and consequences (the queen died of grief). Researchers have dissected the kinds of casual links that make for increased comprehension.

Early work in "story grammars" focused on the primary goals of the protagonist, the obstacles he or she (or it) faces, and the resolution of the conflict. Readers are more likely to recall these "high-level" features than subordinate plots or details of the setting. Subsequent work by Tom Trabasso and Paul Van Den Broek (2002) have refined this model by identifying causal chain in narratives, showing that readers "prune" details that are not part of these chains. As might be expected, comprehension of texts is improved, especially for readers unfamiliar with the topic, when goals are made explicit, when chronological order is maintained, and coherence is tightened (Linderholm et al. 2000).

There are two limitations to this research for the purposes of my argument. First, the texts used by these experimenters are usually very short, direct, often fable-like stories. In other words, they do not pose the same challenges that longer texts pose, particularly those that "mix" genres. So, although they establish beyond question the role of causal links in enabling comprehension, they don't map cleanly onto longer reading passages. And second, they judiciously limit their conclusions to the comprehension of stories.

Comparatively less work has been done on comprehension of expository texts, in part because "exposition" is such a diffuse category (often taking the form of stories), as I have noted earlier. So the question of the role of causality, chronology, and comprehension in expository texts is a much more open question—though given its centrality in comprehension research, we would expect it to have a primary function.

An interesting and important exception is a study by two Spanish researchers, Jose Leon and Gala Penalba (2002), on understanding causality and temporal sequence in scientific discourse. They begin by noting the point I have made previously—that chronological order reflects our natural way of making sense of the world, that we are more comfortable and efficient working from antecedents to consequences. These researchers tested two versions of scientific passages: one that led with the consequence, the death of the river, then moved to the causes; the other preserved chronological order, showing urban pollution leading to the death of the river. In effect, the second was more a story, moving in "natural" time order. Not surprisingly, the authors found the chronological passage easier to understand and conclude that "temporal sequence is a solid criterion to organize causal structures in scientific discourse" (2002, 171). In Chapter 4, we will take this lesson to some textbook passages.

This is not to argue that there are no differences or particular challenges to reading scientific writing. When we read stories, we rarely have to puzzle over the technical terms, and if we do we can usually be confident that a good guess will get us through—not the case in scientific reading. Yet, it would be surprising, given the established fact that causal beliefs are essential for human understanding, that narrative wasn't essential to the comprehension of scientific concepts. Science, after all, is not the description or cataloguing of static features. It is all about motion: evolution, transformation, reproduction, conversion, mutation, survival, living and dying. Nothing is still for long. And the minds we use to comprehend are veritable narrative machines—we dream in stories, remember in stories, create our identities, individual and collective, through stories.

Why would we ever want to leave story behind?

words

Narrative is not a type of writing. Or not merely a type of writing. It has deeper roots than that. It is a property of mind, an innate and indispensible form of understanding, as instinctive as our fear of falling, as our need for human company. Good writers know that and construct plots— itches to be scratched—that sustain us as readers. We are always asking, "What's the story?"

Yet in schools, narrative or story is often compartmentalized ("We do narrative in ninth grade"). Or we treat narrative as purely literary, removed from more practical purposes of persuading and informing. Yet I maintain that we have *literary minds* that seek order by imposing a narrative frame even when we know it makes no sense ("My computer hates me today"). We need this frame for both literary and practical writing. When we employ narratives—and approach experience as *caused* and comprehensible—we gain a measure of control. We take a stand against randomness and fatalism and in favor of a world that makes sense. As creatures living in time, we rely on forms that help us understand our passage through time.

If we accept this conception of narrative—as a foundational mode of understanding—we need to rethink the way we position it in our curriculum.

ITCH AND SCRATCH

CH 3

How Form Really Works

Music takes place in time. . . . it takes time to hear the form.

LEONARD BERNSTEIN, 1964 YOUNG PEOPLE'S CONCERT

In life, conflict often carries a negative connotation, yet in fiction, be it comic or tragic, dramatic conflict is fundamental because in literature only trouble is interesting. Only trouble is interesting.

JANET BURROWAY, ELIZABETH STUCKEY-FRENCH,
NED STUCKEY-FRENCH, *WRITING FICTION*

Nonfiction is currently "sexy." I've seen that claim a number of times related to new attempts to balance literature and nonfiction texts. By *sexy*, I think these commentators simply mean popular or recognized as important; they don't carry that metaphor to the embarrassing lengths that I intend to do. For it seems to me that sustained reading is a mysterious form of attraction—writers inviting readers to stay with them. Readers forming attachments to writers.

Imagine a reader, sitting, still, a book (maybe this book) in her hands. To the outside observer nothing is happening, only the occasional turning of pages, or a short pause to brush back a strand of hair. Yet she continues for long stretches of time; she is, miraculously, *with me*. This extraordinary act of sustained attention cannot be explained on purely cognitive terms, or by the fact that I have a thesis and evidence for it, important as that is. Something more, something embodied, is going on—for if that attraction ever wavers she feels it in her body. She fidgets, yawns, takes a walk. The body is her first-alert system. As a writer, I have to use a variety of resources and appeals to maintain this engagement; I have to be something more than a conveyer of "information."

The writer builds patterns of anticipation and gratification; curiosity and fulfillment; itch and scratch. The great rhetorician, Kenneth Burke, famously defined literary form as "an arousing and fulfillment of desires" (1968, 124). It is the creation of an "appetite . . . and the adequately satisfying of that appetite" through the "sequence" or plot. Surely the sexiest definition of *form* that I know of. In conventional writing instruction, form is invariably confused with formula—all those variants of the hamburger. These give the student no inkling that form has to do something, create something in the reader.

This satisfaction may not come immediately and is often more appealing if there is some delay:

> *This satisfaction—so complicated is the human mechanism—at times involves a temporary set of frustrations, but at the end these frustra-*

NARRATIVES OF OUR READING

Peter Elbow reminds us that reading is temporal—in time, moment by moment. Yet we often represent our reading by a set of categories— voice, organization, correctness—that don't describe well for *what happened* when we were reading. These "static abstractions," as my colleague Bob Connors called them, don't describe the experience of reading. What does a "3" on organization really tell a writer? Does it help him or her understand where there has been a breakdown or problem?

Elbow recommends that to convey this experience we give "movies" of our reading. As we read, what attracted us, pleased us, confused us, caused us to ask questions? Where were we "with" the writer and where did the attraction wane? This is important information.

The primary goal of response, the long-term goal, is to help the writer imagine a reading. Writing, after all, is making reading. To do it well, we have to imagine how a reader might respond moment by moment—and to do that we need to imagine a process, not simply a set of categories. If readers reveal their processes to us, we can internalize or imagine them when we write.

tions prove to be simply a more involved kind of satisfaction, and furthermore serve to make the satisfaction of fulfillment more intense. (Burke 1968, 31)

Elsewhere Burke speaks of feeling the "emotional curve" of a text or piece of music. To be sure, he distinguishes form in scientific writing (which may be driven by curiosity) from literacy form that has "eloquence" and can be repeatedly experienced. Still this concept can be extended to well-written nonfiction to explain how we sustain a reading—though I suspect it would make some cognitive researchers squirm.

Peter Elbow, in his book *Vernacular Eloquence*, extends this concept to all effective writing. Reading, for Elbow, is a matter of moving through time; and good writing "binds time," it gives us the sense of a gratifying sequence, or in Burke's term an experience of "form." But too often we conflate this time-bound experience with a visual representation or shape, which the term *organization* implies:

> *If we want to think better about the organization of temporal media— music, speeches, movies, plays and* writing—*we should avoid words like* shape *and* structure *and* form *with their visual bias. It helps to use a word like* coherence: *it's a word for organization that is not in hock to space. The concept,* organization, *is confused because it conflates two ideas that are quite different: how objects are organized in space and how events are bound in time . . . writing is not a matter of creating timeless logic but of creating sequences of words that* make things happen *in the realm of time.* (2012, 302)

There must be a "pull forward in time." It is more a series of "moves" than a fixed diagrammatic structure.

Writers successfully bind time through "dynamism" through imbuing their writing with energy; in fact, organization should be conceived of as "energy," propelling, inviting, seducing the reader forward. And how is this done?

> *Since reading is a series of events in time, my claim is the same one that applies to music. Successful writers lead us on a journey to satisfaction by way of expectations, frustrations, half satisfactions, temporary satisfactions: a well-planned sequence of yearnings and reliefs, itches and scratches.* (Elbow 2012, 303)

The most obvious way to bind time is to employ a story structure: "Narrative is a universal pattern of language that creates sequences of expectation and satisfaction—itch and scratch" (Elbow 2012, 305).

And Elbow sees narrative as entirely congenial, actually essential, for analytic or academic writing. The very word *essay*, coined by Montaigne, comes from the French word meaning "attempt" and good ones typically show a mind in motion, introducing perplexity, sorting through possible answers, providing a narrative of thought, a mental journey. Even more formal academic essays must establish some problem, itch, or need to read on. Engaging writing often creates the impression (or illusion) of a writer discovering what he or she wants to say in the act of writing, an experience many writers attest to. In his book, *Ignorance: How It Drives Science*, the noted neuroscientist Stuart Firestein challenges scientists to better communicate what they don't know, arguing that this "ignorance" can better communicate the work of scientists:

> Puzzles engage us, questions are more accessible than answers, and
> perhaps more important, emphasizing ignorance makes everyone feel
> more equal, the way the infinity of space pares everyone down to size.
> Journalists can aid in this cause, but scientists themselves must take
> the lead. They have to learn to talk in public about what they don't
> know without feeling this is an admission of stupidity. In science,
> dumb and ignorant are not the same. (2012, 173)

I know in my own science reading, Paul de Kruif's *Microbe Hunters* (now in its 72nd edition!) was an engaging example of science writing as a quest.

The other major tool for sustaining reading is voice. Fiction writers, of course, endlessly comment on finding the right "voice" for a piece—and Richard Ford, for example, will read all of his novels aloud, checking for the sound and rhythm of sentences. He does this though few of his readers will be reading him aloud. Voice is a constant, a human presence, a sensibility, a character, a narrator and guide. Only in a phone book or the equivalent do we get information "raw." But in sustained writing, any information is mediated by a teller, and that teller is part of the reading experience, just as a tour guide is part of the experience of visiting Monticello. When that teller is hidden (often the case with textbooks) or undetectable we have trouble sustaining a reading. The more we sense this human presence, and feel attracted to it, the more willing we are to stay with the text (more on this in Chapter 5).

So What Does All This Mean for Reading and Writing?

If narrative is the deep structure of all sustained writing, and not simply one mode (an easy one at that) among many, the implications for reading and writing are profound. As teachers we can help students unlock the dramatic structure of ideas and information—and they can exploit this drama in their writing. We can, at long last, tell the truth about how exposition works. Here are some first steps:

Looking for Trouble. Tolstoy begins his epic *Anna Karenina* with the famous line: "All happy families resemble one another, but each unhappy family is unhappy in its own way." It follows that unhappiness, some form of trouble, is the starting point for a plot; a character is stifled in his or her situation, or is trying to avoid something, or must confront some loss, or is tempted in some way. Take for example this opening to a recent story by Ben Marcus, "What Have You Done?"

> *When Paul's flight landed in Cleveland they were waiting for him. They'd probably arrived early, set up camp right where the passengers float off the escalator scanning for family. They must have huddled*

*there watching the arrivals board, hoping in the backs of their minds,
and the mushy front parts of their minds, too, yearning with their
entire minds that Paul would do what he usually did—or didn't—
and just not come home.* (2011, 55)

So much trouble here. Paul clearly doesn't want to be here, visiting his
"mushy"-brained family (always referred to as "they")—and, at least in his
mind, he suspects that they would just as soon he didn't come. We learn
that there is a history of them waiting for him, and his failing to show up.
But he's here, and they're here, and the story has a form of propulsion, of
forward movement. How will this encounter play out? What's the back-
story—why this reluctance? We also, in this short opening, have a sense of
how the story will be narrated, from Paul's perspective with full access to
his negative opinions about his family (and himself).

Now let's look at a nonfictional opening, the beginning to Michael Pollan's *In Defense of Food*, a book that would be classified as argumentation:

> *Eat food. Not too much. Mostly plants.*
>
> *That, more or less, is the short answer to the supposedly incredibly
> complicated and confusing question of what we humans should eat in
> order to be maximally healthy.*
>
> *I hate to give the game away right here in the beginning of a whole
> book devoted to the subject, and I am tempted to complicate matters in
> the interest of keeping things going for a couple hundred more pages
> or so. I'll try to resist, but will go ahead and add a few more details
> to flesh out the recommendations. Like, eating a little meat isn't going
> to kill you, though it might be better approached as a side dish than
> as a main. And you're better off eating whole fresh foods rather than
> processed food products. That's what I mean by the recommendation
> to "eat food," which is not quite as simple as it sounds.* (2008, 1)

The same process is at work. There is trouble here as well. Why must this
expert on food tell us that his main recommendation is to "eat food"?
How have we gotten to a place where this is at all controversial or even an
interesting thing to advise us to do? Why is it "not as simple as it sounds"
to do this? What gets in our way of "eating food"? In other words, we have
the beginning to a plot. We have "an itch to scratch."

We also gain a vivid sense of the tour guide we will be traveling with.
Pollan opens with: "I hate to give away the game right here." The "game"?
"Keep things going for a couple hundred pages." "Things"? It's like he is

FROM PETER RABINOWITZ'S "RULES OF NOTICE" IN *BEFORE READING* (1998)

Here is a manageable list of features of writing that call for special notice:

Titles

Beginnings

Climaxes/Key Details

Extended Descriptions

Changes, e.g., in Direction, Setting

Point of View

Repetition

Surprises and Ruptures

Endings

saying, "It's really stupid that I even have to write this book, about something so obvious, but I do." We know what kind of guide or narrator we will travel with—one with a swagger—and I am with him.

Since you are clearly still reading this book, you probably sense that I am trying to follow the pattern I am describing. There is "trouble" in the way we categorize kinds of writing, a conflict between an innate need for narrative structure on one hand—and the claims that we move beyond narrative to more demanding texts on the other. Proposals and research reports similarly follow this kind of pattern—there is trouble there as well: some unmet social problem, or irreconcilable positions in a field of study, or new evidence that challenges accepted views. Articulating this "trouble" is integral to this academic reading and writing.

Take for example, the opening sentence to Jonathan Bate's essay, "The Mirror of Life: How Shakespeare Conquered the World." While less flamboyant than Pollan's opening, Bate's long opening sentence quietly introduces a problem he will then work through:

> *In 1612, around the time that Shakespeare was beginning to work in collaboration with John Fletcher, perhaps as a prelude to his retirement, the young dramatist John Webster wrote a preface to his play* The White Devil *in which he expressed his "good opinion" of the "worthy labours" of his peers in playmaking: the grandiose style of*

George Chapman, the learning of Ben Jonson, the collaborative enter-
prise of Francis Beaumont and John Fletcher, and "the right happy and
copious industry of Mr. Shakespeare, Mr. Decker, and Mr. Heywood."
(2007, 37)

To the modern reader, something feels odd about this list. Shakespeare is given a subordinate position, a seeming afterthought, not even given a full sentence of praise—and the praise given seems to be for his work ethic (a real workhorse, that Shakespeare). How can you square this appraisal with his dominant position today? How and when did he emerge as not only the dominant playwright of his time, but the greatest writer in the language? Well, that is what Bate will set out to explain. The dramatic tension of his essay is coiled in that first sentence.

Consequently, openings should be read very slowly, reread if possible. So much is happening. So many commitments are being made—which is why writers often find them so nerve-racking to write. Openings establish the topic, suggest the problem to be examined, convey sense of the narration and tone of the piece, risking at any millisecond that the reader will go elsewhere. Sometimes when I hear students are taught to write "introductions," I think, "'Introduction?' What is this? A coffee klatch?" There is far more work to be done than "introducing" a thesis; the writer has the much more difficult (but interesting) task of creating the need for the thesis, of setting up the dramatic structure of the piece—one that a reader aligns with, and will stay with.

Identifying the Players. Readers of fiction instinctively begin with the questions: who are the actors and how are they in conflict? We have no interest in reading about the mythical happy families that Tolstoy mentions. Similarly in all analytic writing there needs to be conflicting perspectives, contending solutions, weaknesses and strengths, even good guys and bad guys. If these positions can be attached to spokespersons, so much the better for the drama. Writing is dialogic, involving multiple voices, orchestrated by the author. To comprehend a text is to be attuned to this conflict.

Several years ago I had a reading crisis of my own when I had to teach a graduate seminar in rhetorical theory that spanned two millennia (most programs responsibly break this up into different courses). I had a good anthology but it covered so many diverse writers, intellectual traditions, eras, rhetorical issues, and writing styles that I panicked about where to start. It was educational malpractice for sure. But I began to read with the questions—"Who is this writer responding to? Arguing with? What provoked this writing?" In the seminar we all acknowledged that we were in over our heads, but we dug in and tried to establish this conversation. It's been a lifeline for me ever since.

Attending to Patterns of Thought. Reading, as I am describing it, is not a treasure hunt for the main idea; it is a journey we take with a writer. Gretchen Bernabei encourages her students to make flow charts of the basic *moves* of nonfiction writers to track this movement of mind (2005). Take, for example, a classic text in American history, Martin Luther King's "I Have a Dream" speech. I suspect that we would classify this writing as "persuasion" and not "narrative" if we're into that kind of thing. But to comprehend this great achievement, a reader (or listener) needs to attend to the "plot," even the chronology that forms the spine of his famous speech.

There is trouble from the onset. King invokes the promise of Lincoln and the Emancipation Proclamation but soon sounds a dark note, reminding his audience this promise has not been fulfilled and racial segregation is a fact of life for his race. In this opening he establishes the central conflict of the speech—the gap between the promise of freedom and the realities of racial discrimination. In the middle section he moves to the question of what must be done to get to the Promised Land—particularly the will and discipline needed to resist violent confrontation. And in the final, best known, part he describes what the Promised Land will be. To comprehend the speech, I would argue, is to be attuned to this construction of tension and resolution, something we miss when we only get the uplifting and better-known conclusion. Moreover, the speech is located in history, moving from past, to present, to imagined future.

Two Absurdly Simple Rules for Reading and Writing

If we had to pass on advice, under the limitation of twitter characters, here would be my advice for writers and readers:

1. *Read as if it is a story.*
2. *Write as if it is a story.*

More than ninety characters to spare.

I suspect it is the first piece of advice that is most unusual. Reading, it is now claimed, *is* "rocket science," complicated beyond the capacity of most mortals to understand. But it makes basic sense to read dramatically, even when what we read does not easily fall into any dramatic genre. Of course, we can read plays and novels, biographies, memoirs, even many poems as stories—but commentaries, reports, arguments, analyses? That seems a stretch.

Yet we can dramatize just about any text. We can ask what is at stake. What problem, issue, "trouble" is prompting the writing? What needs to be solved? What are the contending positions or alternatives? Readers may have to build some of this friction themselves, supply one or more of these alternatives, introduce a naysayer. If you are only given one unchallenged point of view, someone is trying to pick your pocket. We can ask: what are the consequences of the idea or proposal? Are there unintended consequences not specified? In other words, ideas, even abstract ones, are developed through a series of actions. Good writing has a sense of motion, pace, anticipation, and I would argue "plot." Critical reading is all about friction—trouble.

Unfortunately, students, as I have noted earlier, are often taught a static and nondialogic version of exposition; the perennial five-paragraph theme. In their influential small text, *They Say/I Say: The Moves That Matter in Academic Writing*, Gerald Graff and Cathy Birkenstein point out the problem in the conventional school essay:

> *Too often . . . academic writing is taught as a process of saying "true" or "smart" things in a vacuum, as if it were possible to argue effectively without being in conversation with someone else. If you have been taught to write a traditional five-paragraph essay, for example, you have learned to develop a thesis and support it with evidence. This is good advice as far as it goes, but it leaves out the important fact that in the real world we don't make arguments without being provoked. We make arguments because someone has said or done something (or perhaps not said or done something) and we need to respond.* (2007, 3)

Graff and Birkenstein do something that my writing teachers never managed to do—explain what a "good thesis" is. What situation in the novel *called for explanation*? What problem was my writing to solve? This sense of provocation is the link to what I call *drama* or *plot*. *Provocation* implies a tension, a friction, a puzzle, an incompleteness, a need to have our say. If we're only saying, "Me, too" or "I agree," endorsing what everyone believes, arguing for the obvious, making no "news," there would be no call to continue the conversation. Nothing is caused. The resolving of this tension and our response to this provocation propels the narrative motion—the plot—of argument. Good arguments *feel* dramatic, and sometimes, when they speak back to common sense and accepted wisdom, they can be exhilaratingly liberating.

The Journey to the Thesis

We can undermine critical thinking by treating the thesis, stated early, as the key to an effective argument—not because the thesis is unimportant, but because we need to teach students how to get to a thesis, to create a need for a thesis in the first place, *and how to write toward it*. What question, problem, does the thesis solve? It took me literally years, and many mediocre papers in college, before I sorted this out. I knew I had to *have* a thesis, that I had to support it, but I was clueless about what constituted a "good" thesis. I felt like I was spinning my wheels defending claims that never got me above a C+. There were some tacit criteria that I couldn't figure out. My problem wasn't that I failed to support my claim; it was that my claim solved no problem, at least no interesting problem.

It would have been different if I had been taught by my brilliant colleague Gary Lindberg who invited students to second-guess the decisions of characters, to look at choices they made and imagine alternatives. Here is one of his prompts:

> For each character involved, describe what the character could *say or could do in the scene but chooses* not to. *Explain as clearly as you can why the characters behave as they do. Do you see any unspoken rules or habits or patterns that are guiding them?* (1986, 150)

This is a wonderfully generative prompt that disrupts the inevitability of the text—could it have happened differently? Suppose we apply it to *The Great Gatsby* and take the incident where Daisy and Gatsby are returning to Long Island after the disastrous hotel confrontation where they confront Daisy's husband Tom about their plans. On the way back Tom's mistress, Myrtle Wilson, thinking Tom is driving, rushes in front of the car and is instantly killed, but the car never returns to the scene. We get two accounts—one from an observer:

> The "death car," as the newspapers called it, didn't stop; it came out
> of the gathering darkness, wavered tragically for a moment, and then
> disappeared around the next bend. (Fitzgerald 1925/2003, 144)

And later in the day, we get Gatsby's own account that he gave to Nick Carraway:

> "Was Daisy driving?"
>
> "Yes," he said after a moment, "but of course I'll say I was. You
> see, when we left New York she was very nervous and she thought it
> would steady her nerves to drive—and this woman rushed out at us
> just as we were passing a car coming the other way. It all happened in
> a minute, but it seemed to me that she wanted to speak to us, thought
> we were somebody she knew. Well, first Daisy turned away from the
> woman toward the other car, and then lost her nerve and turned back.
> The second my hand reached the wheel I felt the shock—it must have
> killed her instantly."
>
> "It ripped her open—"
>
> "Don't tell me, old sport." He winced. "Anyhow—Daisy stepped
> on it. I tried to make her stop, but couldn't so I pulled the emergency
> brake. Then she fell over into my lap and I drove on." (151–52)

Gatsby makes two major judgment calls in this account, both revealing. He acquiesces in allowing Daisy to drive to "steady her nerves," when given the turmoil of the hotel scene, one might have expected him to convince her otherwise.

But the major one is to go on, not to return to the scene of the accident, a crime even at that time. Once he brought the car to a stop, he could have reversed direction and gone back to the scene. One obvious reason would have been to shield Daisy from responsibility, but he could have done that by driving back himself and admitting that he was at the wheel at the time of the collision. Another might be to avoid any legal responsibility, to really hit and run, but here too he seems to assume he will have to account for his action (i.e., claim to be the driver), so that explanation doesn't work.

What in his character or his pattern of behavior prevented him from doing the ethical thing at this point? This, is seems to me, is an interesting problem worth exploring.

He may have intended to go back, when he stopped the car, but then changed his mind when she "fell over into [his] lap." Perhaps at that moment he seemed to possess her, as he had dreamed all along, and nothing else existed for him. In fact, by the time he talks with Carraway he really doesn't want to hear anything about Myrtle or the accident, he blocks it out of his mind, and his sole concern is about Daisy. After recounting the accident he says about Daisy:

> *"She'll be all right tomorrow," he said presently. "I'm just going to wait here and see if he tries to bother her about that unpleasantness this afternoon." (151–52)*

It is as if the fatal accident with Myrtle has ceased to exist, at least in his consciousness. He brushes it aside as "unpleasantness." Nothing exists except Daisy, and he expects that she too will be able to banish the accident from consciousness and be "all right tomorrow."

Carraway makes an interesting decision in this scene, as well. He is clearly disgusted with Gatsby's indifference—but he doesn't reveal this reaction to Gatsby; and he chooses not to tell Gatsby that the accident had been witnessed. He explains himself this way: "I disliked him so much by this time that I didn't find it necessary to tell him he was wrong" (151).

This feels illogical. The stronger you feel about something, the less likely you are to say something? Is he saying that he is so alienated from Gatsby that he won't even commit himself to conveying this critical information, that it is not worth the effort? Do we trust Carraway's self-explanation? Or might his motive have been different—that he was still so much in awe of Gatsby that he could not confront him?—and do we see that passive, submissive streak elsewhere?

Even as he wrote this scene, Fitzgerald was playing with alternatives. The handwritten first draft (now digitally available from the Princeton archives) shows some of these changes. In the original, Gatsby's admission was written this way: "Well, Daisy was driving but we've agreed to say I was" (Facsimile 212). In the final version, the implication was that the decision was solely Gatsby's. He can appear the gallant rescuer that he imagines himself to be.

The most intriguing change from manuscript to final version occurs when Gatsby stops the car, and it involves just one word. In the original Daisy falls into his "arms"—an almost conventional romantic moment. But in the final version she falls into his "lap"—a difference any teenager would see as significant. Is it surrender? Sexual submission? Manipulation? Your call.

Lindberg's prompt asks if this decision reflects in any way a "pattern"—are there other instances where Gatsby's single-minded focus on Daisy prevented him from accepting responsibility for his actions? One obvious example is his relationship with Meyer Wolfstein and the fixing of the 1919 World Series—one assumes Gatsby benefited financially from that. We might also add the scene previous to this the accident where Gatsby insists Carraway and Jordon Baker witness the brutal hotel scene where Daisy announces she is leaving Tom, oblivious to the effect it might have on them (was it a cause of Carraway breaking the relationship at the end of the book?—another good question I think).

At the end of the book, Carraway finally pronounces judgment on the Buchanans:

> *They were careless people, Tom and Daisy—they smashed up things and creatures and then retreated back into their money and their vast carelessness, or whatever it was that kept them together, and let other people clean up the mess they had made.* (188)

But wasn't this true of Gatsby as well, with his ability to compartmentalize, to banish from his mind the literal act of smashing Myrtle's body, and then driving on to leave others to deal with her mangled body? To help fix the World Series and then move on. Isn't there a moral carelessness there too, and if so, what do we make of Carraway's judgment that Gatsby is better than all the rest? Do we trust it? Do we accept the "great" in the title of the book?

One question enchains another, so the project of analysis is not simply an act of being bound by a thesis but of opening up new questions. They invite more conversation. By looking carefully at one scene (and not just finding quotes for a broad thesis), we can help students find a keyhole to begin analysis, working out from the issues and "trouble" they will find there—if they read carefully. Another virtue is that it doesn't ask students to make broad sociological or philosophic claims that (a) they lack knowledge to make and (b) take them away from the specific action and behavior in the novel. Instead they rely on our intuitive resources, what Rabinowitz and Bancroft call "mind reading" (2014). What is in Daisy's mind when she puts her head on Gatsby's lap? What's in his? And do they match?

I am not contending that literary analysis or argument looks like narrative fiction. But arguments that sustain reading must have a dramatic core, a plot. Like a good piece of music, there needs to be a pattern of tension and resolution, problem and solution, anticipation and fulfillment. When done well, the sensation of reading doesn't feel like we are working in a tightly contained form, tyrannized by a thesis, the stern father who sits at the head of the table and rules over all. Rather, we feel a mind at work; the sensation is of a journey that may take us to a thesis but invites new questions along the way.

STORIES OF OUR THINKING

Gretchen Bernabei has done wonders to open up the possibilities for expository structures—which she calls "stories of thinking" (2012). In other words, the structure of the writing mirrors the act of coming to understanding. *It enacts thinking*. As readers we are able to follow a mind at work.

But how do we turn the standard five-paragraph "antiperplexity" machine into a perplexity machine? Bernabei would suggest we find other templates or structures to do this.

Here is what I would propose for the literary analysis papers that remain central to writing in English classes.

1. Describe a scene or situation in a text that raises an interesting question.
2. What is that question?
3. What are some possible answers to that question?
4. Which is the most compelling answer to that question?
5. How does this new understanding of the situation help you understand other parts of the book?

This sequence leads to an inquiry-based paper, not one driven by an opening thesis.

As I've thought about story structure and the presentation of information, I've begun to pay special attention to how reports are presented to our local school board, which I joined in 2012. One heavy duty of a board member is to take in information from presentations—and since our meetings are televised we all *have* to look interested. And sometimes we are. The reports that sustain our attention have form—as I have described it here. They work when there is an issue, a tension, a problem, a need to improve some aspect of our schools. Something is at stake, our high school is bleeding energy, high school students are electing not to take math courses in their senior year. The presenter then shows how this issue could be resolved, perhaps ending with a recommendation. We are on a quest.

The presenters who lose us fail to do this—they fail to create any palpable sense of anticipation. Or drama. For example, they may begin with a long description of how a committee was formed. Crucial information is mixed with irrelevant data. We all *feel* this formlessness, and just hope to hide our reactions from the cameras.

Form, I am convinced, is not simply a structure or plan or outline; it is a deeply embodied invitation to movement.

PART 2

THE **ART** OF INFORMING

inspiration

plot

build

conviction

THE SEVEN DEADLY SINS OF TEXTBOOKS

Read proudly—put the duty of being read invariably on the author.

RALPH WALDO EMERSON, SPEECH AT CONCORD LIBRARY DEDICATION

In this time of raising standards, it's appropriate to ask if the standards for writing textbooks might also be raised. In this time of promoting "text complexity" and reading "difficult" texts, it might also be wise to ask if student difficulty (and boredom) comes from poor writing, from what Walt Whitman called "twistified or foggy sentences." I see the failure of textbooks all the time at my university, often around exam time.

The note cards come out.

Pairs of students will be huddled together with a wad of note cards with key terms on them. The cards often seem to be in no particular order, and the result is sheer, brute and brutal, isolated memorization. Perhaps there are acronyms or mnemonics that help with this memorizing, but rarely, so far as I can see, a fitting of these terms into a pattern that might enable real learning. I suspect the names and terms don't last long in the students' memories. When I was in school I swear that I could *feel* the information leaving my head after an exam.

It will come as no surprise that I will claim that there is poor writing, and this poor writing is caused by the consistent failure to employ narrative effectively. We crave causal patterns—actors and consequences—and when we don't get them our reading processes break down, our attention fails.

We also crave vividness—details that ground ideas in specifics, taste, touch, images, metaphors.

But there is more at stake than a simple argument about style. The formal written, expository language (clearly the language of textbooks) represents reality as stable, solid, observable, and measureable. There are permanent and enduring truths, represented in sentences like this one:

> *The conversion of hydrogen to helium in the interior of stars is the source of energy for the immense output of heat and light.* (Elbow 2012, 83)

We instantly recognize this sentence as written in the textbook style. The *is* conveys a sense of incontrovertible certainty or "crystalline" stasis. This conception of physical reality is challenged by modern physics—and a more process-like form of writing better captures this changing conception. Indeed science is all about change over time, and not simply the static properties of life and matter. This more kinetic view of science demands a language closer to speech, with an emphasis on process and action.

Peter Elbow rewrites the sentence on hydrogen to capture the dynamic, process-like quality of the assertion:

> *When stars convert hydrogen into helium at their cores, they get the energy they need for putting out so much light and heat.* (Elbow 2012, 83)

Here the stars are actors, in motion, even with "needs." Elbow is less interested in the theoretical claims about science than in the ways we can employ speech resources in writing, and one of the key resources is story—the representation of reality as plotted, as involving agents, actions, and consequences:

> *Language usually gets its meaning into the minds of listeners or readers when it involves movement or change through time. Putting this crudely: stories tend to help us experience a meaning better— even a conceptual meaning—than purely conceptual language.* (Elbow 2012, 99)

We work better with a dynamic world that *happens*, than a stable world that *is*.

Realists might claim that it is futile to finger textbooks as the culprit—they are here to stay, they are fixtures, and their style of writing is as permanent as the bolded terms that announce what must be learned. Cynics would argue that textbooks are not really "read" in the first place. It is pointless to show how "difficult" passages can be rewritten for better comprehension.

But I will argue in this chapter that this "rewriting" is what we have to do mentally to make sense of that difficulty. Even if this criticism affects nothing in the textbook world (probably a safe prediction), we can identify practices that habitually cause comprehension difficulties. The problem is not always our failure to handle complex texts. We need to mentally repair the writing so we can understand it—in this way reading is a form of rewriting. I also worry that textbook language be taken as a model for students' writing of informational texts. We can do better than that.

Let's take as an example, the following passage from the McGraw-Hill/Glencoe textbook, *Biology*, which would be used most likely in a twelfth-grade science class. The passage describes how mutation aids in the survival of bacteria. We'll look at just the first two sentences.

> **Mutations.** *If the environment changes and bacteria are not well-adapted to the new conditions, extinction of the bacteria is a possibility. Because bacteria reproduce so quickly and their population grows rapidly, genetic mutations can help bacteria survive in changing environments.* (Biggs et al. 2007, 522)

This is not terrible writing, but I suspect it is not totally clear to students. I suspect the term *environment* will be too abstract for many as it is used in a more specialized way than it normally is. But the real problem sentence, in my view, is the second one:

> *Because bacteria reproduce so quickly and their population grows rapidly, genetic mutations can help bacteria survive in changing environments.*

It doesn't directly pick up the idea of extinction. Linguists would say that coherence in writing comes from picking up the idea of the previous sentence (the *given*) and following it with the *new* information. Here would be my rewriting:

> **Mutations.** *Bacteria may become extinct if their environment changes—becomes warmer, for example, because of climate change. When this happens they may fail to adapt. But bacteria regularly avoid extinction because they reproduce frequently, sometimes every*

*fifteen minutes, increasing the odds that they can create mutations
that help them survive.*

I would immodestly claim that my version is superior, if not vastly so.
It is more specific: it defines the features of the environment that might
cause extinction and it gives a figure, easily available, on how frequently
bacteria reproduce, a detail that has what James Kinneavy (1971) called
"surprise value." My version is also tighter on the central point, the story,
of causality—that changes in environment threaten bacteria and that
mutations help them survive. In general my version is more active, with
active verbs replacing less vigorous "to be" verbs.

It should be noted, in fairness, that textbook writers and those who
create reading tests operate with someone looking over their shoulder,
actually inquisitors from all parts of the political spectrum—what Diane
Ravitch (2003) calls "the language police." Should Cesar Chavez be
included? How can you finesse a description of evolution for the Texas
Book Selection Committee? What do you do with climate change? It is
commercial good sense to smooth out or avoid altogether any controversies, to the point that censorship becomes self-censorship. In Ravitch's
view, this makes for bad history, also bad writing.

In this chapter, I will examine seven tendencies in textbook writing that
are used consistently, to the point that they define a *style* of writing, even
a representation of reality. For each I will point out how these tendencies
create difficulty for readers. I illustrate these difficulties with passages that
I see as representative. In some cases, I will explore how they could have
been rewritten for greater comprehensibility, often by exploiting narrative,
dramatic, and descriptive tools.

Sin #1. Flatness. By *flatness*, I mean the seeming refusal to create human
interest, often in events that were tremendously interesting. In her study of
history textbooks, Frances Fitzgerald notes that textbook titles often claim
to deal with motion and story—*The Land of Progress: The Rise of the American Nation.* Yet she finds these titles "ironic" because the texts, by covering
so much in chronological order, feel "static."

> *Because the texts cannot identify the actors in history, they cannot
> make these connections. Events—wars, political disputes, judicial
> decisions—simply appear like Athena out of the head of Zeus. And
> history is just one damn thing after another. It is in fact not history at
> all.* (1979, 161)

Textbooks that have appeared since Fitzgerald's critique are even more fragmented, as they seem to cater to lower reading and attention levels of students. It is rare for a student to read more than three paragraphs without a section head shifting topics. Textbooks take on a *People* magazine look.

Take for example this two paragraph section, "China Under Mao," from the Glencoe/McGraw-Hill text, *Human Heritage: A World History* that would most likely be used in a late middle school or early high school world cultures class:

> *Mao's main goal was to make China a strong, modern country. In 1953 the Chinese began a series of plans to improve the country's economy. By the middle of the 1960s, the Chinese had more food and better health care. Many people had learned how to read and write. Also, under Mao the position of women in China changed. Women were now allowed to choose their husbands, enter into any occupation they chose, and receive equal pay. Men, however, continued to hold the highest positions in government and the best paying jobs.*
>
> *Then Mao began to fear that the Chinese had lost their revolutionary spirit. As a result, in 1966 he carried out **purges**, or removals of undesirable members of the Communist party. He also purged the country's intellectuals, or scholars. This purge was called the Cultural Revolution. Students and young adults known as the Red Guards attacked politicians, teachers, and others accused of not supporting communism. The purge soon got out of control, however, and there were battles between Red Guards and other citizens. The Red Guards were later broken up.* (Greenblatt and Lemmo 2001, 630–31)

It is difficult to imagine a blander description of one of the most epic (and tragic) transformations in world history. Mao comes across as a neutral agrarian reformer, when in fact these reforms caused suffering and death on the scale that Stalin inflicted on the Soviet Union—more than 36,000,000 people died in the Great Famine of 1958–1962 because of Mao's reforms (Johnson 2010)—equivalent to one of every nine people in the United States today. A "series of plans to improve the economy" indeed. Educator and historian Diane Ravitch notes that even in texts that acknowledge these facts, "it often seems as though these are just unfortunate events that occurred while Mao and the Communist party were successfully transforming China into a modernized society" (2003, 144).

And we have a language of euphemism that seems straight out of Orwell: "got out of control," "removals of undesirable members." Even the one really active verb *attacked* is left vague and undramatic, a missed opportunity. And the whole passage ends limply and passively: "The Red Guards were later broken up." How? By whom?

One might argue that the space limitations, and the oh-so-obvious adherence to readability levels, are a cause here, but what prevents the writer from including a sentence on what happened to the purged people? On how they were publicly humiliated by having to wear dunce caps, signs around their necks, and often forced to confess their "crimes" in public squares before being executed? On the unbelievable human costs of Mao's reforms? Any reader of quality children's nonfiction picture books knows that brevity is no excuse. The function of this writing, I feel, is to be a bearer of names, of facts. A wagon. And for that very reason it fails in its task—because it is so unmemorable, even untrue.

Sin #2. Overuse of "To Be" Verbs and Passive Constructions. In his classic text on style, Joseph Williams makes a basic statement how active verbs contribute to a vigorous, readable style. I have already quoted it but it deserves an encore:

> *A clear and direct style depends first on how we express action. As we'll use the word here, action will cover many notions: movement, feeling, process, change, activity, condition—physical or mental, literal or figurative. The important point is this: While we cannot always express action in a verb, in the clearest and most vigorous sentences, we usually do.* (1981, 9–10)

The major culprits in a "nonactive" style are the passive sentences—where there is no agent or actor—and the linking "to be" verb.

So let's put another description from the Glencoe/McGraw-Hill *Biology* text to the test. In this passage, the authors describe the role of amino acids in building body proteins:

> *During the process of digestion, proteins in foods are broken down to their subunit amino acids. The amino acids are absorbed into the bloodstream and carried to various body cells. Those body cells, through the process of protein synthesis, assemble the amino acids into proteins needed for body structures and functions.*

Humans require 20 different amino acids for protein synthesis. The human body can synthesize 12 of the 20 amino acids needed for cellular function. Essential amino acids are the eight amino acids that must be included in a person's diet. Animal products, such as meat, fish, poultry, eggs, and dairy products, are sources of all eight amino acids. Vegetables, fruits, and grains contain amino acids, but no single plant food source contains all eight essential amino acids. However, certain combinations, such as rice and beans, shown in Figure 35.9 provide all of the essential amino acids. (Biggs et al. 2007, 1027)

Although serviceable, this passage feels repetitive and passive. One sentence is particularly egregious:

Essential amino acids are eight amino acids that must be included in a person's diet.

Surely we can do better than that:

The other eight—called essential amino acids—must be part of our diet.

So here is my rewrite:

When we digest food, enzymes help break down proteins into subunits called amino acids. The bloodstream then absorbs these amino acids and carries them to various body cells where they are reassembled into proteins needed for body structures and functions. Since many of our body proteins have a life span of hours or days, this renewal is crucial.

Humans can synthesize or create twelve of the twenty amino acids needed for protein synthesis. The other eight—called essential amino acids—must be part of our diet. Animal products, such as meat, fish, poultry, eggs, and dairy products, can provide all eight essential amino acids. Although no single plant source provides all eight, combinations such as rice and beans can provide all of the essential amino acids.

The major change is that I provide agents for the actions described. Rather than proteins being passively broken down, I introduce the agent—enzymes. I make the bloodstream active by absorbing the amino acids. I change *contain* to the more active *provide*. I also add a fact—again easily available about the life span of proteins, which establishes the urgency of protein reproduction. All in fewer words.

John Dewey also found that in the writing of children, this active style, which highlighted causality, was a key indicator of understanding and engagement. He quotes from a student notebook on geological and geographic study:

> When the earth cooled, calcium was in the rocks. Then the carbon dioxide and water united and formed a solution, and, as it ran it tore out the calcium and carried it to the sea, where there were little animals that who took it out of solution. (1971, 58)

Dewey then comments on this student writing: "I call this language poetic, because the child has a clear image and a strong personal feeling for the realities imaged." He stresses the active verbs like *tore*, showing a chain of causation, as evidence of learning or what he calls "personal realization."

Sin #3. Piling On. This sin consists of simply overloading the reader with terms and names and in the process obscuring the relationships or sequences that might make this information coherently memorable. Hence the note cards. Often there is failure to use verbs in a compelling way that would make the action or "story" understandable for the reader.

I include as an example one more passage (the last I promise) from *Biology*. It is from a section on the immune system dealing with specific immunity, described as a second line of defense against "pathogens"—the first being "nonspecific" defenses like the skin and mucus, which form barriers. The second line of defense includes white blood cells and inflammation, which protect the body when specific pathogens invade the body. Here's the passage. Take a deep breath and read it:

> **Lymphatic organs:** *The organs of the lymphatic system contain lymphatic tissue, lymphocytes, a few other cell types, and connective tissue.* **Lymphocytes** *are a type of white blood cell that is produced in red bone marrow. These lymphatic organs include the lymph nodes, tonsils, spleen, thymus gland, and diffused lymphatic tissue found in the mucous membranes of the intestinal, respiratory, urinary and genital tracts.*
>
> *The lymph nodes filter the lymph and remove foreign particles from the lymph. The tonsils form a protective ring of lymphatic tissue between the nasal and oral cavities. This helps protect against bacteria and other harmful materials in the nose and mouth. The spleen stores blood and destroys damaged red blood cells. It also contains lymphatic tissue that responds to foreign substances in the*

blood. The thymus gland, which is located above the heart, plays a role in activating a special kind of lymphocyte called T-cells. T-cells are produced in the bone marrow, but they mature in the thymus gland. (Biggs et al. 2007, 1086)

Tough going—right?

I find these two paragraphs virtually incoherent because they embed so many lists. The first paragraph has three: the contents of the lymphatic organs, the list of organs, and the location of these organ systems. The ordering of the lists also seems off—one would expect the naming of the organs to come first, before information on what they contain. Furthermore, the bolding of *lymphocytes* actually threw me off, as I expected the paragraph to focus on that term, which isn't mentioned again until the end of the next paragraph.

Similarly the second paragraph presents a daunting list that would be better comprehended if presented in bulleted form. The reader, I feel, also needs some reminding that the function of this list is *protection* (and the passage fails to explain how T-cells perform this protective function). So here would be my revision:

> *The organs of the lymphatic system are located throughout the body. They include: lymph nodes (we have about six hundred, mostly in the armpits and groin), tonsils, spleen, thymus gland, and diffused lymphatic tissue found in the mucous membranes throughout the body. These organs contain lymphatic tissue, lymphocytes, a few other cell types, and connective tissue—and all serve to purify and protect the human body.*
>
> *These organs protect us in various ways:*
>
> - *Lymph nodes remove foreign materials (e.g., bacteria and viruses) from the lymph.*
> - *Tonsils form a protective area of lymphatic tissue between the nasal and oral cavities, which keeps harmful matter in the nose and mouth.*
> - *The spleen stores blood and destroys damaged red blood cells.*
> - *The thymus gland, located above the heart, helps activate a special kind of lymphocyte called the T-cell (T for thymus). The T-cells are like soldiers who search out and destroy the targeted invaders.*
>
> *These organs enable our bodies to identify and attack specific pathogens or threats to the human body.*

In my view, it is much easier to process lists if they are presented this way; it is much harder if lists are embedded in continuous paragraphs. But even my revision has problems—will students know how crucial lymphocytes are to our immune system, when they are just a name in a list?

AVOIDING OFFENSE

Textbook writers work with constraints similar to test makers; that is, they have to navigate controversial topics to avoid having their efforts rejected. As Diane Ravitch (2003) has documented, they face censorship from both ends of the political spectrum—or just from concerns about student discomfort.

But recently the New York City schools took "niceness" to a new level. In a Call for Proposals for the new reading tests, a range of topics and words were considered inappropriate: they would be troubling or cause "distraction" when students are taking the test. These included: *dinosaur, birthday, pepperoni, dancing* (with the exception of ballet), *space aliens, Halloween, divorce, disease, home computers, slavery.* Over fifty of them.

Who would have thought that these city kids would be so fragile?

Sin # 4. Refusal to Surprise. It is possible to be too sober. To never let down your guard. To fail to let a ray of humor lighten a piece of writing. Yet the best nonfiction writers I know are constantly on the lookout for the odd, quirky, surprising fact that can humanize writing. I remember as a kid, I couldn't get enough of Ripley's Believe It or Not! books. I absorbed stories like that of Joseph Kissinger, who in 1960, to test survivability in an aborted space mission, ascended in a hot air balloon to an altitude of 20 miles, then parachuted, reaching a speed of 614 miles/hour (close to the speed of sound) before opening his parachute—and survived. I couldn't get enough of that. The kid's science magazine *Ranger Rick* is a wonderful source of such facts. For example, in a chart on animal heartbeats you get the contrast between a mouse (650 beats/minute—over ten per second!) and a hibernating groundhog (three beats/minute).

According to James Kinneavy, "'information' in a statement consists in the degree of improbability of the statement. 'Information' is news, and news is the unpredictable, the unforeseen, the improbable" (1971, 93). If I tell you that the sun came up this morning, that would convey no news, unless perhaps some apocalyptic community had predicted the end of the world that night. Real news activates us as readers—we physically feel a small jolt of energy from the unexpected fact.

While the previous passage on China tiptoes around any arresting facts, some textbook writers do a much better job. The value of this surprise is evident in this textbook account of home construction in Levittown, one of the first post-WWII suburbs. It is taken from *The American Nation* (Davidson, Stoff, and Viola):

> Because these houses were mass-produced, they cost much less to build than custom-made houses. They could also be constructed rapidly. Using preassembled materials, teams of carpenters, plumbers, and electricians could put up a Levitt house in 16 minutes. (2003, 845)

This final stunning statistic does vital work. It impresses on our memory the degree of simplicity and uniformity in these houses. And I would even argue that it helps the "ethos" of the textbook writer(s)—they care about maintaining our interest; they share our affection for the strange and improbable.

Sin # 5. Lack of a Point of View. In *The Language Police*, Diane Ravitch is scathing in her criticism of the style of much of the writing in history textbooks:

> Their tone—that ubiquitous, smug tone of omniscience—seems to come from the same word processor, the one that writes short declarative sentences and has a ready explanation for every event in history. . . . Instead of presenting conflicting views and letting students debate ideas, the textbooks tell them what they are supposed to believe. (2003, 149)

Ravitch's concern is the presentation of history; mine is readability. But this toneless, noncontroversial quality of writing leads to both bad history and voiceless writing that is entirely unmemorable. As Donald Graves often remarked, it is writing where "no one is home." The reader is never addressed; the writer is hidden. By assuming a tone of assured factuality and certainty, the writing disguises its own bias.

It is writing that perpetuates the mythology of "facts" and goes something like this: facts are solid, verifiable, "true." Opinions on the other hand are suspect and challengeable, tainted by bias. Virtually every curriculum guide I know encourages students to make this distinction (and in the wider culture it leads to claims that evolution is "just a theory").

But facts must be located and chosen, and these very acts introduce a bias. Facts are *used*; they are employed in discourse, and that very use introduces bias. There's no escaping it. Truth is perspectival, partial, contestable; there is no view from everywhere, at least none that humans can attain. To the extent that writers address a reader, make clear the argumentative nature of their claims, readers can be part of a dialogue and debate. But when that bias is hidden or muted, reading becomes more passive and acquiescing, less dramatic—and I would argue more difficult.

Here is the kind of writing that Ravitch is targeting. It comes again from Glencoe's *Human Heritage: A World History.* Admittedly this is a lot to cover in any textbook, but brevity cannot justify the passive way the history of the Vietnam War is presented. Here is the complete account:

> *A war for control of the country erupted between South Vietnam and North Vietnam. Guerillas, known as the Vietcong, and the Soviet Union aided North Vietnam. The United States had already been sending military supplies to South Vietnam. It began sending troops there in 1965. Altogether, more than 3.3 million Americans fought in Vietnam. Eventually 58,000 of them lost their lives, and almost $200 billion was spent.*
>
> *The Vietnam War deeply divided the American people. Many believed the United States should fight to help South Vietnam and prevent the spread of communism. Many others believed the fight was a civil war that the Vietnamese should settle for themselves.*
> (Greenblatt and Lemmo 2001, 628)

The obvious omission here is the failure to include any statistic on the exponentially greater loss of life among the Vietnamese people—about 900,000 by the most reliable estimate. Recall this is a "World History." This omission sends the inaccurate message that the United States suffered the most in this war. The 58,000 figure is "true," but misleading, as it fails to account for non-American suffering.

The writing is stunningly passive, as if history occurs with no agents: the war "erupted"; "$200 billion was spent"; the United States just began sending troops for no stated reason. Things happened. The only hint of the divisiveness came in the two opinions about the war, which the writers don't even begin to unravel. I'm convinced that whoever wrote this really didn't really want to touch the subject.

Sin #6. The Refusal of Metaphor and Analogy. A few years ago, I was working with a third-grade class on family sayings. We asked each of the students to interview a family member and come back with a saying that is repeated so often that it becomes part of the family rituals. Often the best ones came from grandparents, like "Does it look like I fell off a turnip wagon?" In other words: how stupid do you think I am? Like most sayings, it grounds something that is abstract, stupidity or gullibility, in a miniature story. We imagine a dull peasant, a rube, who couldn't even manage to stay on the wagon, an easy target for more sophisticated town-dwellers.

Metaphors work as ministories, translating something new and complex into more manageable scenarios. The persistent prompt is "What is this like?" Metaphors link the new to the known—we picture DNA as a twisting ladder, as code, as containing lethal genetic time bombs. I have already quoted textbook descriptions of the immune system, and I will contrast them with some descriptions by Jerome Groopman, a cancer researcher and physician, author of *How Doctors Think* (2008) and *The Measure of Our Days* (1997), an account of his work with gravely ill patients. Here is how he describes the function of white leukemic blood cells:

> *Regardless of the setting, the behavior of the leukemic cell is that of a pernicious sociopath. The mutation in the genetic blueprint radically changes the temperament of a normally courteous white cell. The transformed primitive white cell, called a "leukemic blast," becomes grandiose and aggressive. It grows without restraint in the bone marrow, inconsiderate of the needs of fellow blood cells. The marrow is soon congested with the bullying leukemic blasts. The normal blood cells are crowded out and fail to develop.*
>
> *But the leukemic white cells are not satisfied with simply overrunning the bone marrow and elbowing out their normal brethren. They are like a gang of punks on a wilding spree, and race through the bloodstream, invading and damaging organs like the liver and brain.* (1997, 92)

Compare this description to that of *Biology*:

> *Cancer is characterized by abnormal cell growth. Normally, certain regulatory molecules in the body control the beginning and ending of the cell cycle. If this control is lost, abnormal cell growth occurs that could lead to various types of tumors as shown in Figure 37.16.* (Biggs et al. 2007, 1093)

The difference could hardly be more stark. Groopman creates an extended metaphor comparing mutated cells to sociopaths, bullies, thugs. There is vivid action here—congesting, elbowing out, over-running, crowding, damaging. There is an unfair conflict between the normal "courteous" cells, and the "grandiose and aggressive" mutated ones. There is drama, story—all of which helps us understand the deadliness of leukemia. By contrast, the textbook language avoids metaphor by adhering to passive, even euphemistic, constructions ("is characterized by"; "If this control is lost").

There is clearly reluctance on the part of textbook writers to cross the line into metaphor; it may sound too literary, too "authored"—or metaphor may seem suspect because all of them are "wrong" in some way. Cancer cells are only like "sociopaths" in some ways, like thugs in some ways. They don't have intentions, they are not legally responsible for their actions, they don't stand around street corners in menacing ways. Still, the connection, flawed as all metaphors are, helps us to imagine their destructiveness.

Analogies are the near-cousin of metaphors, as they explain a novel concept in terms of a well-known action or experience. Here is how Temple Grandin explains her rejection of a simplistic view of "locating" cognitive functions and behavior in specific parts of the brain:

> Researchers also can't assume that if a patient is exhibiting abnormal behavior and the scientists find a lesion, they've found the source of the behavior. I remember sitting in a neurology lecture in graduate school and suspecting that linking a specific behavior and a specific lesion in the brain was wrong. I imagined myself opening the back of an old-fashioned television and starting to cut wires. If the picture went out, could I safely say I had found the "picture center"? No, because there are lots of wires back there that I could cut and make the TV go blank. . . .
>
> The picture depends not on any one specific cause, but on a collection of causes, all interdependent. And this is precisely the conclusion that researchers in recent years have begun to reach about the brain— that a lot of functions depend on not just one specific source, but a large network. (In Groopman 2013, 41)

This is great teaching, drawing on an experience that most readers can easily imagine. But rarely do we get this kind of grounding in the language of textbooks.

Sin # 7. Ignoring the Human Need for Alternation. Readers have difficulty with texts that fail to shift mood, register, level of seriousness. The very word *monotonous* captures our reaction to a single (mono) tone. Seriousness creates a need for humor; logical development creates a need for story; formality creates a need for colloquial expressions; and as noted previously abstraction creates a need for metaphor. We can't stay in one place for too long, we have to move. A number of the examples I have included illustrate this tendency.

As readers we are gratified by what Ken Macrorie (1985) called "alternating current," the fusion of high and low discourse, sophisticated language and street language, the mind and the body (more on this in the next chapter). We can see it in H. L. Mencken's famous definition of *puritanism*: "the haunting fear that someone somewhere may be happy" (1959, 626). We move from the elevated diction "haunting fear" to the punch line, the more colloquial "happy."

Peter Elbow makes a strong case for the value of "speech inflected writing" that moves into and out of the language of casual speaking. Take this section from an essay by Paul Krugman on technology and climate change:

> *It's even possible that decarbonizing will take place without special encouragement, but we can't and shouldn't count on that. The point, instead, is that drastic cuts in greenhouse gas emissions are now within fairly easy reach.*
> *So is the climate threat solved? Well, it should be. (2014)*

The obvious speech interjection is "Well." Krugman could have omitted it, and maintained a more *written* style, but this bit of speech makes his writing—and him—more accessible.

And to be fair, some textbook writing exploits this principle of alternation as well. To demonstrate I will rewrite a paragraph from Prentice Hall's *The American Nation* that describes the suburbanization that occurred post–WWII. Here is how it might have read:

> *As millions flocked to the suburbs, central cities began a slow decline. Suburbs and shopping centers drained cities of businesses and taxes. Since most of those who moved were white, this change segregated the races.*

Not terrible, but also not particularly memorable. But here is what the authors (and the book *does* feel authored) wrote:

As millions flocked to the suburbs, central cities began a slow decline.
Suburbs and shopping centers drained cities of businesses and taxes.
Since most of those who moved were white, some critics complained
that the Unites States was turning into a nation of "chocolate cities
and vanilla suburbs." (Davidson, Stoff, and Viola 2003, 845)

That final metaphor is memorable, and unexpected.

There are to be sure other ways of creating alternation: the occasional short sentence or well-placed fragment; the parenthetical aside to the reader; the illustrative anecdote; the well-chosen quote; the comic twist. All of them, if well placed, make the reading of information writing and analysis manageable, even rewarding, to a reader. By contrast, we can feel the lack of alternation and variety in our bodies; we *feel* "monotony" before we can understand the reason for it. In short, we are made to move.

It might be objected that I am simply trying to turn textbooks into creative nonfiction and that entertainment was never one of their primary functions. Their purpose is to convey information in a straightforward way. But I am accepting that premise, or at least that intention. And I am arguing that these so-called creative techniques will help in the retention of information. They satisfy a human need for causality, for fitting information into patterns, sequences, narratives; they present us with a world in motion, with actions and consequences—not one of unconnected "facts." These strategies also pull back the curtain on the telling; they present us with a narrator, a human presence that is acting as our guide. These are, then, not simply stylistic tricks. They are strategies for helping us retain what we read.

ALL WRITING IS NARRATED

In most books, the *I*, or first person, is omitted; in this it will be retained; that, in respect to egotism, is the main difference. We commonly do not remember that it is, after all, always the first person that is speaking.

HENRY DAVID THOREAU, *WALDEN*

What really knocks me out is a book that, when you're all done reading it, you wish the author that wrote it was a terrific friend of yours and you could call him up on the phone whenever you felt like it. That doesn't happen much, though.

J. D. SALINGER, *CATCHER IN THE RYE*

We typically think of the "narrator" as a feature of fiction. This narrator may be reliable or unreliable—or some degree in between. The narrator may be omniscient or have limited access to information. But the undeniable fact is that we experience fiction through the mediating lens of a narrator, a teller.

But isn't this the case with all writing? As readers, we are never face-to-face with raw reality, whatever that might look like. Information of almost any kind comes to us through some teller, some guide, and some authorial presence. Even very young writers know this and often take the role of tour guide, ushering us through their information: "Hello. My name is Emily and I am going to tell you about different kinds of cats." One of the reasons we sustain a reading is our willingness, even pleasure, in being in the company of this teller.

The situation is similar to teaching a class. Years ago, during a discussion of course organization, my colleague Brock Dethier made an insightful point. He said that the primary organizing feature of the course was the style or temperament of the teacher. His or her humor, voice, manner of questioning—these consistencies of behavior and personality—were at least as crucial for providing continuity as a well-constructed teaching plan. That's why a substitute teacher feels so disruptive, even when following the regular teacher's lesson.

This *I* that a writer creates is not an authentic and complete presentation of self (whatever that might look like). Rather, as in teaching, it is a performative role that makes use of our personalities and temperaments—we reveal some things about ourselves and withhold other things. The "writing self" I try to present is a better version of myself: more confident, more knowledgeable, more caring, more assured, more upbeat, better humored than I actually feel a lot of the time. When I am asked to speak about a book I have written, I'm tempted to say, "No, just stay with the self in the book. He's better than I am."

In this chapter, I explore the ways nonfiction writers establish an "ethos" or a "persona" that a reader will stay with. Much of this obviously has to do with the subject—it doesn't take much of a writer to interest me in the hiking trails of the White Mountains, or the swimming exploits of Missy Franklin. But if I am to sustain a reading, even on those topics, a writer has work to do. I need to feel confident that he or she can keep me engaged, that the writing can have momentum and energy and attractiveness and often personality. Kenneth Burke (1968) claims that literature creates an "appetite in the mind"—and I would say that good nonfiction does the same.

So what's the trick? How is it done?

To even ask the question may be to commit to too big a topic. This sustaining of engagement, this deployment of an authorial presence, constitutes a major skill of writing. I can only scratch the surface, but scratch I will. In this chapter, I will focus on how writers establish this engaging presence—in the next I will look at the larger "plots" they create to maintain engagement. But before I dive in, a short digression on *attention*.

If the goal of reading nonfiction is to retain what we read—a reasonable assumption—attention is crucial, for we generally don't retain things we don't attend to. That's plain common sense. In fact, most of what we do, see, read is forgotten, and for good reason. If we remembered everything, our circuits would be overloaded. As readers, the best we can do is skillful attending and skillful forgetting; as writers we need to invoke (arouse?) attention in such a way as to keep a reader with us and shape the reading so our key ideas are remembered (though what strikes a reader might not be what we think is most significant). No attention, no comprehension. And "the more attention the brain pays to a given stimulus, the more elaborately the information will be encoded—and retained" (Medina 2008, 125).

Textbook writers, of course, know this and direct our attention to **bolded** terms (i.e., this will be on the test). But by the hundredth term, this is only tedious. And willpower, forcing ourselves to pay attention, can take us only some way. Without some help from the writer, we wear out and start skipping. William James, in his *Talks to Teachers on Psychology* (1958), warned about relying too much on what he called "voluntary attention," the conscious efforts we make to focus. These efforts, he says, can come only in spurts or pulses; they involve paying attention to our difficulty in paying attention ("Boy, I've lost concentration").

We are at our most efficient, he claims, when we are not focused on attention, but on the subject of our attention (he calls this spontaneous or "passive" attention). He offers some guidance on how teachers can elicit this passive attention: "The prescription is that *the subject must be made to show new aspects of itself; to prompt new questions; in a word to change*" (79). And he offers good advice for teachers (and I would add writers) to maintain attention:

> If the topic be highly abstract, show its nature by concrete examples. If it be unfamiliar trace some point of analogy in it with the known. If it be inhuman, make it a figure as part of story. If it be difficult, couple it with some prospect of personal gain. Above all things make sure that it shall run through certain inner changes, since no unvarying object can possibly hold the mental field for long. (84)

In other words, there need to be some *plotting*, some patterning of change, in the presentation of any material. One of my colleagues, a physics teacher, claims that in his lectures there needs to be a "narrative arc" to maintain student attention. No variation, no motion, no attention, no comprehension.

Here are some other principles I will explore in this chapter that can keep our attention:

- We attend to incidents, facts, language, statements that surprise us, that do not fit our normal pattern of expectations.
- We attend to situations where we have an emotional or personal stake. For example, we need to see the human consequences of scientific advances.
- Attention requires variation. Whatever state we are in calls up an appetite for an alternative state. Sitting creates a desire to stand; seriousness, a desire for laugher; generalizations, for specifics— and so on.

Nothing surprising about this. We travel, we take vacations, to disrupt our own routines, to create memories, and often we can recall these trips day by day. New experiences, even unpleasant ones (sometimes especially unpleasant ones) stay with and give us the satisfaction of a life that can be recalled. Reading and writing are a form of travel, through time, and writers need to create the conditions for attention. And to reiterate a theme of this book, *the tools and skills we normally associate with literature are essential to maintaining attention, and enabling comprehension and critical thinking*.

Reasons to "Stay with Me"

Humor. Writers do not need to be comedians, but it surely helps to inject humor into almost any topic. A capacity to mock the seriousness of any situation or position is a sign of mental health—and to be too much in the "role," to be humorless and over serious, is actually unnerving for those around such a person. The sociologist Erving Goffman (1961) coined the term *underlife* to describe how we undercut the seriousness of the social roles we take—stepping back from them momentarily. He describes the way doctors and patients at St. Elizabeth's Psychiatric Hospital would use humor to mock their position; for example, patients would develop elaborate rituals to pretend to take their medicine. Doctors would occasionally pretend to be patients. We see underlife at work at "roasts" where the conventional rules of respect and status are dropped. Goffman saw this undercutting humor as essential to human functioning in social organization.

Let's begin with the comic aside, often taking the form of a comment in parentheses. Of course, the greatest use of parentheses has to occur in *Lolita* where Humbert Humbert gives this account of the death of his mother:

> *My very photogenic mother died in a freak accident (picnic, lightning) when I was three, and save for a pocket of warmth in the darkest past, nothing of her exists within the hollows and dells of memory.* (Nabokov 1955, 12)

His mother's death doesn't even merit a full sentence.

As you may have noticed I have an affection for this form of aside as it provides a way of seeming to add something new or slightly unexpected, as in this sentence that I hope you have already read, where I comment on the five-paragraph theme:

> *I have since heard this model referred to as the "hamburger" format with the opening and closing paragraphs being the two buns and the body being the meat. This has always seemed to me not only a disservice to students, and to nonfiction writing, but also an insult to hamburgers—because they, after all, have more variety than that (double-cheese, bacon burger, pretzel burgers, even burgers with the fries in the bun).*

The parentheses here allow me to take the issue to a point of absurdity, as if I am defending the good name of hamburgers.

Michael Pollan is an artist of the parentheses. In his book, *In Defense of Food*, he describes how food loses nutrients, but not calories, in the act of shipping:

> *In general, calories are much easier to transport—in the form of refined grains or sugar—than nutrients, which are liable to attract the attention of bacteria, insects, and rodents, all keenly interested in nutrients. (More so, apparently, than we are.)* (2008, 97)

This last comment is wonderfully ironic, showing that even bacteria have a better food sense than humans.

Parentheses can also allow the writer to double back and mock himself or herself, as an act of underlife, which suggests not taking oneself totally seriously. Here is Jon Young in his wonderful book, *What the Robin Knows*, describing how songbirds use chain link fences for protection:

*While feeding or just hanging out, they can work both sides of the
fence, confident that, should the time come, they can dive through
a convenient link to perfect safety. If the attacker isn't ready for the
fence, the unexpected encounter could be painful. Shaking its head
and preening his mangled feathers, the Cooper's [Hawk] may mutter
to itself* Nobody saw that right? *(Egregious anthropomorphism, I
admit.)* (2012, 151–52)

Young's aside seems to say to the audience, "Just having fun here. Letting
my imagination go. Hope you understand."

Of course parentheses are only one tool. Maybe the quality I am trying
to describe is a sense of delight in the absurd or paradoxical, a sense of
irony, what has traditionally been called *wit*, which serves to lighten the
topic. I have to restrain myself from quoting more of Pollan (there are also
copyright limitations), so as an example let's go back to Thoreau himself
and this devastating bit of irony about vegetarianism in *Walden*:

*One farmer says to me, "You cannot live on vegetable food solely, for
it furnishes nothing to make the bones with"; and so he religiously
devotes a part of his day to supplying his system with the raw material of bones; walking all the while he talks behind his oxen, which,
with vegetable-made bones, jerk him and his lumbering plough along
in spite of every obstacle.* (2000, 43–44)

One of the great modern science writers, Lewis Thomas, could also employ
an unexpected ironic twist, as in this passage where he describes the plight
of the microbe that causes human illness:

*Pathogenicity may be something of a disadvantage for most microbes,
carrying lethal risks more frightening to them than to us. The man
who catches a meningococcus is in considerably less danger for his life,
even without chemotherapy, than meningococci with the bad luck to
catch a man.* (1974, 90)

Pity the vulnerable microbe!

This attraction to irony can also enliven the writing of students, as in this
comment by one of my first-year college writers on the shifting attention
spans of young media users:

*Convinced that kids these days spend way too much time inside star-
ing at screens, I take them outside. We play baseball for five minutes*

before dropping the bats and gloves and moving on to street hockey in the driveway. From there we spend as much time suiting up Brendan in the goalie equipment as we do shooting on him. Following this pattern, the kids promptly drop all the gear and move on to the next activity. The attention span of kids these days really does astound me. Any game that requires more than two minutes of preparation or doesn't reward them in some way within the next five is a waste of their time. Even something as basic and necessary as eating bores them. What kind of generation of children are we raising that gets bored of eating? (Greg Magni)

For me this last line, that even eating bores these kids, shows the comic absurdity of having to be entertained all the time.

What does a writer gain by this use of humor and wit? Paradoxically, it helps establish "ethos" and credibility. It is a sign of confidence that a writer can be funny, even mildly so—which is why inexperienced writers regularly fail to try it. It shows a sensitivity to readers who can be weighed down by seriousness; it offers a break, a respite, "relief" in the classical sense. We can take a breath. We are taken care of. These comic moments, these ironic observations and asides, also reassure a reader by mocking human self-importance and overconfidence, even as a writer works to be serious. For we *can* be serious without being solemn.

Surprise Value. A close cousin of humor is surprise—in fact, humor is a form of surprise. As we have observed in previous chapters, "surprise" is an essential characteristic of information. Writers can also delight us by the well-chosen, unexpected fact. Take for example Evan Osnos' description of female attendants on high-speed Chinese trains:

The guests are ushered aboard by female attendants in Pan Am-style pillbox hats and pencil skirts; each attendant, according to regulations, had to be at least five feet-five inches tall, and was trained to smile with exactly eight visible teeth. (44)

This last qualification is, for me at least, completely unexpected (I mean who does the counting?) It's a setup. We expect some height qualification, and we are prepared for another similar kind of criteria—but not visible teeth. This one detail provides a spark of energy to the account; like humor, it enhances the credibility of the author who has shown he can notice the odd detail or fact that can make his point.

Popular science writers are typically alert to the energizing fact or statistic. Here are two examples drawn from the 2011 anthology, *The Best American Science and Nature Writing*, the first from a piece by Stephen Hawking and Leonard Mlodinow called "The (Elusive) Theory of Everything":

> *A few years ago the City Council of Monza, Italy barred pet owners from keeping goldfish in curved fishbowls. The sponsors of the measure explained that it is cruel to keep fish in a bowl because the curved sides give the fish a distorted view of reality. Aside from the measure's significance to the poor goldfish, the story raises an interesting philosophical question: How do we know the reality we perceive is true?* (2011, 186)

This lead does marvelous work, as it anchors a complex theoretical question in the odd decision of the Monza City Council. Not only does it show that the writers have a sense of ironic detail—it assures us that they won't lose us in theory.

The surprising statistic can also startle, as in this example from Jill Sisson Quinn's essay, "Sign Here If You Exist," in which she challenges our view that we are a biologically autonomous "self":

> *Most parasites do not kill their hosts. You—your living, breathing self—are evidence of this, as you host an array of parasitic microbes. . . . The majority of these microbes are mutualistic, meaning that both you and the microbe benefit from your relationship. A whopping 3.3 pounds of bacteria, representing five hundred separate species, live inside your intestines. You provide them with the suitable environment—the right moisture, temperature and pH—and feed them the carbohydrates that you take in. They shoot you a solid supply of vitamins K and B12, and other nutrients.* (2012, 275–76)

These numbers are stunning—3.3 *pounds* of bacteria, equivalent to the weight of a small pot roast—in our intestines, living mutually within us. Again, we feel gratified by this surprise.

Employing Speech. One obvious way of conveying an authorial presence is to shift from a more formal written register into a speech register—as Quinn does when she uses the adjective *whopping*. Shifts like these create comfort, intimacy, even a momentary sense of relaxation—as if to say, "I know this is science, but it's really not that complicated. See, I can talk about it with everyday language." Again, it gives a reader a sense of confidence. The sense of alternation also creates a feeling of momentary surprise—and as I have argued earlier, alternation, in this case downshifting into a colloquial register, is critical to sustaining attention.

Here is an attempt I made earlier in this book to inject a speech feature in my writing. I wanted to comment on the circularity of claims about informational writing:

> It is a truism, a circular and almost unquestioned belief, that we read informational writing for . . . , well, information.

I wanted to introduce an almost confused pause as if someone were trying to come up with a definition and fails.

We can see this downshifting at work in a tenth-grade paper on the Common Core State Standards website. It is an amazing timed essay on the evolution of Napoleon's character in *Animal Farm*. One of the criteria for evaluating this writing is that it "establishes and maintains a formal style and objective tone." This is bad advice in my view, a recipe for boredom, enforced monotony. The evaluators claim, rightfully, that the student does maintain this tone of formality. But with one "exception," one lapse that occurs in the following excerpt:

> Being power hungry always causes problems, and boy did Napoleon cause problems. The animals had received so little food that many were starving; you could see their bones, and some even died of starvation. (2010b, 68)

The one lapse is clearly "and boy did Napoleon cause problems." *Boy* is the problem.

But is this really a flaw? Or a good intuition on the part of the writer, that a shift to a colloquial expression would add energy to the piece, that it would reflect his own engagement with the topic? Would the piece have been better if he had written: "And Napoleon clearly causes problems"? Not in my view. I like the original better. We see this downshifting all the time in effective writing, and it works to create that mysterious quality called voice.

We don't have to go far to find established columnists committing the same lapses, as in the case of a pre-election column by Paul Krugman:

> Lately, however, I've seen a growing number of Romney supporters making a quite different argument. Vote for Mr. Romney, they say, because if he loses, Republicans will destroy the economy.

O.K., they don't quite put it that way. The argument is phrased in
terms of "partisan gridlock," as if both parties were equally extreme.
But they aren't. (2012)

It's the same deal; Krugman introduces the colloquial "O.K." and a shift
in register, which raises the question of why a tenth grader should have to
write in a more formal style than Paul Krugman.

One of my own students, Crystal Gosnell, expertly shifts from a "written" register to a spoken one in this account of her regret at inheriting her
father's nose—and not her mother's:

> *My mother's nose slopes down from her forehead in a perfect curve*
> *on both sides; unbelievably symmetrical and slender at the bridge and*
> *comes to a subtle halt in the form of a perfect, cartilage point. Not bul-*
> *bous and wide, but soft and elegant. It suits her face and adds a little*
> *something to her—it doesn't command her features or draw attention*
> *to itself. She doesn't have The Gosnell Nose.*
>
> *I can't tell you how many times people have said to me upon meet-*
> *ing both of my parents—where the hell did you come from? They say*
> *I kinda look like my mom but not really. That I sorta look like my dad*
> *but not really. Except for the nose. They say you have your father's*
> *nose. Every. Single. Time. I'm aware, thank you.*

There is a clear downshift in the second paragraph, signaled by the word
hell. After an elaborate description of her mother's nose in the first paragraph, we are suddenly in the world of speech ("kinda," "sorta," "Every.
Single. Time") ending in a direct, and annoyed, address to those who comment on her nose.

Another obvious way to downshift to speech is quotation, a critical skill
for science writers who rely on experts to explain their work. The well-
chosen quote often provides a jolt of energy, a crystallization, as in this
example from John McPhee's *The Control of Nature* in which he explores
the ways people have tried to control the path of the Mississippi River:

> *If people were to farm successfully in the rich loams of the natural*
> *levees—or anywhere nearby—they could not allow the Mississippi to*
> *continue in its natural state. Herbert Kassner, the division's public-*
> *relations director, once remarked to me, "This river used to meander all*
> *over the floodplain. People would move their tepees, and that was that.*
> *You can't move Vicksburg."* (1989, 32)

This perfectly chosen quote allows for a shift from McPhee's more formal (written) language ("continue in its natural state") to the spoken language of the quotation ("and that was that").

Affection for Material. As I have mentioned earlier, my father was a biologist whose fascination with man-biting mosquitoes developed during World War II when he was stationed in New Guinea and the Philippines. After the war he took a position at Ashland College where he taught biology.

As I began to read some of his favorite texts, I could see that his mentors did not hide their affection and fascination. One of them was Karl von Fritsch, who described how bees use dances to communicate the location of a feeding place, a "round dance" for closer blossoms, a "waggle dance," for more distant sources. Here is his description of the "round dance":

> The foraging bee . . . begins to perform a kind of "round dance." On the part of the comb where she is sitting she starts whirling around in a narrow circle, constantly changing her direction, turning now right, now left, dancing clockwise and anti-clockwise, in quick succession, describing between one and two circles in each direction. This dance is performed among the thickest bustle of the hive. What makes it so particularly striking and attractive is the way it infects the surrounding bees; those sitting next to the dancer start tripping after her, always trying to keep their outstretched feelers on close contact with the tip of her abdomen. . . . They take part in each of her manoeuvrings so that the dancer herself, in her mad wheeling movements, appears to carry behind her a perpetual comet's tail of bees. (1966, 102)

I love the great verbs—the dancer *infects* the other bees that *start tripping after her.* Von Fritsch's fascination with his topic is palpable.

Nature writers live by this credo, and convey a sense of affection, awe, and respect for the subject of their investigations. It is more than conveying "information": it is an attitude, a point of view, a deeply personal relationship to the life-forms, processes, and material they explain. Here is Jon Young, again, describing the proper way to approach a "sit spot."

> Actually, the best time to don your keen awareness is before you enter the sit spot. The owl doesn't leave its roost and just blunder blindly into the trees, and the cat does not leave its porch for the bushes in a hurry. From the silent and invisible perch, the owl surveys the

landscape with those incredible eyes and listens with ears that are
as remarkable as the deer's. It sees and hears the squirrels, the mice,
the deer crunching the leaf litter, the muskrat digging and feeding, the
rustle of the wind blowing in the sedges and the cattails. You could do
worse than emulate the owl. (2012, 61)

We can point to clear word choices, mainly verbs, that help us imagine
the attentiveness of this owl—and establish the voice and presence of
the author. But it is more than that—there is an ethic being conveyed, of
the mutuality of life-forms, of the dazzling skills at play in the nonhuman
world. The owl, even the familiar robin, can be our mentors.

Grounding the Complex in the Familiar. Another form of downshifting
occurs when we explain an abstract concept in terms of something more
familiar—as von Fritsch does when he describes the dancing bees as a
"comet's tail." I can think of no writing skill more important than this one.
It is at the core of the Christian explanation of religious faith in the gospels,
which include some of the most familiar stories we know. Recall that Jesus
in these gospels is trying to convey a sense of a newly abstract monotheistic
god to an audience more familiar with more concrete local gods, represented by idols or icons. His strategy is to make abstract qualities (God's love)
present to his hearers through parables as he does in the case of the story
of the shepherd and the lost sheep that appears in the Gospel of Luke:

What man of you, having a hundred sheep, if he has lost one of them,
does not leave the ninety-nine in the wilderness, and go after the one
which is lost, until he finds it? And when he has found it, he lays it on
his shoulders, rejoicing. And when he comes home, he calls together
his friends and neighbors, saying to them, "Rejoice with me, for I have
found my sheep which is lost." Even so, I tell you there is more joy in
heaven over one sinner who repents than over ninety-nine religious
persons who need no repentance. (Luke 15:3–7)

Unforgettable, and for Christians eternally reassuring.

Writers, as they compose, are constantly self-prompting, provoking
ourselves to think through our material—*and a central prompt is "What is*
this (idea, situation, feeling, process) like?" What familiar image or story can I
use to ground it; how do I connect the new to the known?

This instinct for the right analogy or metaphor helps establish ethos and
confidence in the reader—especially valuable in popular science writing

where there may be some anxiety on the part of the reader, memories of being lost in college lectures, defeated by complexity and terminology. Here, for example, is Malcolm Gladwell (surely the most widely read nonfiction writer going) on the evolution of leukemia treatment in the 1950s, when cancer researcher, Emil Friereich, began to design treatments using drugs in combination, a process that had worked earlier in combating tuberculosis:

> *Their solution was to use multiple drugs simultaneously that worked in very different ways. Friereich wondered about applying that model to leukemia. Methotrexate worked by disrupting folic acid uptake, which was crucial in the division of the cells; 6-MP shut down the synthesis of purine, which was also crucial in cell division.* (2011, 161)

I suspect that at this point Gladwell realized that he was pushing the bounds of a reader's capacity for taking in technical information. So he pauses for an analogy:

> *Putting the two together would be like hitting cancer with a left hook and a right hook.* (161)

We feel assured that we get it—and assured that Gladwell, like any good teacher, will keep us with him.

One of my favorite examples of this process occurs in George Orwell's classic essay "Politics and the English Language" where he is describing a downward spiral in which muddled language produces sloppy thinking, which makes for even more muddled language:

> *An effect can become a cause, reinforcing the original cause and reproducing the same effect in intensified form, and so on indefinitely.* (2002, 954)

Had Orwell proceeded at this level of generality, he might have lost us on the opening page of the essay. But he clinches his point in an analogy:

> *A man may take to drink because he feels himself to be a failure, and then fail all the more because he drinks. It is rather the same thing that is happening to the English language.* (954)

We say, "OK, I get the cycle he is referring to." He is attentive to our need for a concrete reference point for his idea.

We get the same expert grounding in the children's science book, *I Face the Wind*, where the author Vicki Cobb (2003) helps readers understand how wind, though invisible, has force. It's a difficult concept even for adults—as we see trees bending to some invisible power. Cobb depicts a young girl rolling a ball against her leg, slowly first and faster the second time. "Which makes the stronger bump?" the text asks. A molecule of air is like a tiny ball that depending on velocity exerts the same kind of force. This invisible wind is like that—tiny balls hitting us at different speeds. It makes sense.

Strategic Self-Disclosure. Through the examples in this chapter I have tried to show a few ways authors create a reliable, engaging presence—one that we will want to travel with. Not all of these strategies involve the first person, but some like "testimony" do. The inclusion of personal testimony can backfire and seem self-involved and digressive. But if the disclosure is relevant to the topic (and well told), readers typically appreciate it; testimony established the writer's credibility and authenticity. That was what I was trying for in the opening to my last book, *The Art of Slow Reading*, which I began this way:

> *I am a slow reader. There, it's out.*
>
> *I can imagine few readers, not even my family members, who will want to read an entire book about my reading process. And this is not such a book. But my own slowness is clearly a motivation for writing. It may take me a week to read a book that, a colleague assures me, I "can read in a night." I've even bookmarked comic books.* (3)

I wanted to "out myself" as a slow reader, to use myself as an example, and to begin to turn what had long seemed to be a disability into a strength, hoping that other slow readers would identify with me. Thoreau reminds us of the power of testimony in his opening to *Walden*:

> *I on my side require of every writer, first or last, a simple and sincere account of his own life, and not merely what he has heard of other men's lives; some such account as he would send to his kindred from a distant land; for if he has lived sincerely, it must have been in a distant land from me.* (2000, 39)

It is a conventional academic move to brand testimony as "anecdotal" even softheaded and sentimental, a sop to the reader. If we were made of sterner, more rational stuff, we could make decisions and learn information more objectively. But we simply do not work that way.

I call a shift like this a *move*. Nonfiction, I will argue, is all about *moves*, motion through time. Not static structures. And skilled writers have a repertoire of moves that strategically invite the reader along. I recall vividly a short conversation with the great nonfiction writer John McPhee, whom I have already quoted. He has just published his acclaimed book on Alaska, *Coming into the Country*, and after a reading he had a reception at the house of a faculty member. When my turn came to talk to him, I asked about the length of his paragraphs. Did any editors force him to divide them? ("Yes," he said. "Like breaking knees.") But then he said, "In some pieces there is a point when you need a long paragraph, like in my book, *A Roomful of Hovings* (1968). Let me show you."

He looked for some paper, then noticed the windows of the house. It was winter outside and they were all covered with condensation. McPhee went up to the picture window and began using it as a blackboard, depicting the structure of his book. "You see, I have two different narratives in the book that come together at this spot. And here I need a big paragraph to pull the narratives together." He marked that spot with a big X on the window. I realized how dynamic and experimental structure was for him, how he was aware of moving us to that crucial paragraph.

If all works well, we are carried forward as we read, sustained, seduced by the writer who may, herself, have felt this motion in the act of writing— as the topic seemed to open up, as she "listened to the text" that at times seemed to take on a life of its own. Of course, we do plan ahead, but if we are responsive to what we are doing, it we are really listening, new opportunities continue to present themselves. We are not simply passive, and accepting; we are using this evolving text to prompt ourselves.

Writers have internalized a set of self-prompts that allow the writing to continue, often in ways that were not expected at the start—and fluency is all about the operation of these prompts. Here is a list of the ones I would see as central (or at least central to me):

1. *What happens next?*
2. *What does it look like, feel like, smell like?*
3. *How can I restate that?*
4. *What's my reaction to that?*
5. *What example or experience can I call up to illustrate that?*
6. *What's my evidence?*

7. What parts of my prior reading can I bring to bear on that?

8. What comparison can I make that makes that clearer?

9. Why does that matter?

10. What do I mean by that?

11. Who else would agree with that? Disagree? What would they say?

12. How can I qualify my statement? What are the exceptions?

13. How does that fit into larger debates or controversies?

Collectively questions like these can create a sense of movement, flow, consecutiveness. One thing we do in writing conferences is to demonstrate these prompts through our questions—and they then go "underground" and become part of the writers subconscious process, as scaffolding theory would suggest.

The teller, narrator, writer invites us on a cognitive journey, an unfolding, a quest. When done well, the writer provides welcome shifts that keep us from being in one place too long: humor punctuates seriousness, example follows assertion, and the colloquial mixes with the formal. And because we can continually reuse these prompts, because they are not used up like an outline, writers can feel the fullness of their topics—or as Montaigne said, he could continue his essays "as long as the world has ink and paper" (1987, 1070).

words

In this chapter, I have tried to extend the theme of this book, that so-called "literary" qualities of writing—such as narration—are not mere aesthetic features, confined to literature. All writing is narrated; it comes through a teller, a mediator, a guide who must win our trust, and in some cases wins affection. As writers we are asking something extraordinary: that readers keep going by choice and not out of duty. In my view "information" is not enough of an incentive, unless we are writing a pure reference book. One of our indispensible tools is . . . ourself. Not the self, maybe, that today might be whining about the abrupt early November snowstorm outside my window. But a self we craft—a better me, smarter, craftier, wittier, more nimble, more confident self that invites you, the reader, to stay with me.

ON MISS FRIZZLE'S BUS

Or, How We Really Want to Learn Science

"Time to move," said Hermit Crab one day in January.

ERIC CARLE, *A HOUSE FOR HERMIT CRAB*

One memory that unites many of us baby boomers is watching *Hemo the Magnificent* in junior high school. The fact that each school had to obtain a 16-mm film reel makes this an even more impressive achievement. It was created in 1957 by Bell Labs, produced by Frank Capra, opened with the music of Beethoven's Ninth, with state-of-the-art animation, and narrated by "Dr. Research" Frank Baxter. It taught us more—lastingly more—about the circulatory system in fifty-five minutes than any other source we would come up against.

I recently revisited the film's ending, set to the final chorus of the Ninth Symphony, with Baxter listing all we don't know about the circulatory system ("How's this for ignorance?") as the film ends on a close-up of a beating heart. When it was first shown, *Time* magazine panned it for dumbing down the science, but even at the time I thought it was the model for how I wanted to learn. Many of us still remember Baxter's quick comeback when Hemo (the great animated character representing the heart) challenges him to name the common substance that most resembles blood—and he answers "seawater."

I expect that if today's students, a few decades into the future, recalled their elementary science learning they might recall The Magic Schoolbus series, and the eccentric Miss Frizzle with her uncontrollable red hair, thermometer earrings, and science-themed dresses. She is the obsessed, eccentric, unconventional teacher we all like to remember. The books typically begin inside the school; kids have done research, made charts. But, to this point the learning is static, almost purely verbal, conventional. Then the trip starts, into the ocean, down in the earth's interior, to prehistoric times, with Miss Fizzle fearlessly driving the bus. The books not only convey information; they give us a taste for inquiry—science, they tell us, is about getting on the bus and moving.

I draw a couple of conclusions from *Hemo* and The Magic Schoolbus. First, we like to learn science from an enthusiast so that we catch the spirit of inquiry as well as the information. How this information is *mediated* is important. And some degree of eccentricity helps, as with Bill Nye the Science Guy; in other words, we learn what it is like to have an intellectual passion. And second, we like to get on the bus. We like the movement of inquiry, puzzles to be solved, explanations to be discovered. When information is part of some quest, some problem to be solved, we have a schema for taking it in, and a dramatic structure for maintaining attention, for "binding time." In this chapter I want to look at how skilled science writing, from Eric Carle to *The New York Times*, gets us on the bus.

To Read to the End: Writing About Cancer for *The New York Times*

If we were to select consequential science writers, ones whose job is to explain critical, potentially lifesaving medical advances to a broad public—we might well start with Denise Grady. Her job is to understand and explain some of the most complex medical research for the readers of *The New York Times*. Her pieces are often long, requiring readers to make the always-tricky move from a front page to the continuation inside the paper—so, as she explains it, one of her major tasks is for readers to "read to the end," to suppress or defeat our tendency to read extractively. I'll take one of her most complex pieces, "An Immune System Trained to Kill Cancer," to show her subtle use of narrative to convey an important medical discovery.

Grady, like many science writers, likes to begin with a case to help frame the information that will follow: "I use narratives whenever I can because they keep people reading them. We all want to find out what happens next, how it turns out. So when I can I try to find a story and some interesting characters, and use them as a framework for the rest of the information I'm trying to get across." She does exactly this in her article, which begins with a leukemia patient who seemed out of options:

> *Mr. Ludwig, then 65, a retired corrections officer from Bridgeton, N.J., felt his life draining away and thought he had nothing to lose.*
>
> *Doctors removed a billion of his T-cells—a type of white blood cell that fights viruses and* tumors*—and gave them new genes that would program the cells to attack his cancer. Then the altered cells were dripped back into Mr. Ludwig's veins.*
>
> *At first, nothing happened. But after 10 days, hell broke loose in his hospital room. He began shaking with chills. His temperature shot up. His blood pressure shot down. He became so ill that doctors moved him into intensive care and warned that he might die. His family gathered at the hospital, fearing the worst.* (2011)

Grady comes up with the startling fact that the treatment killed off "two pounds" of cancer cells.

With this personal hook established, she can move into the more technical part of her article, explaining how this altering of the immune system is engineered. And here again, she makes use of several story schema or analogies familiar to readers. The patient's T-cells are "reprogrammed" to find and attack the cancerous B cells (part of the immune system); and they use as a "target" the protein CD19, which is on the surface of B cells. In the words of the principle researcher, Dr. Carl June, the inserted protein complexes turn these T-cells into "serial killers."

The tough question remains—how does the modified DNA get into the T-cells, and here the answer is surprising. Dr. June and his associates used a "gutted" version of the HIV virus that can enter the cells but is disabled from reproducing as it would if it were full-blown AIDS. The patient's T-cells are removed, any remaining T-cells in the body are killed (so as not to impede the treatment), the T-cells are exposed to the vector or carrier (the doctored HIV virus) and reinserted into the patient. At this point Dr. June claims, "The patient becomes a bioreactor." Another helpful analogy.

The modified T-cells can then attack the body's B-cells. (It kills both cancerous and noncancerous cells—so the patient will need medication to help with the infections B cells normally control.) So step-by-step Grady takes us through the most technical part of her article, aided by a

ARTICLE OF THE WEEK

All writing, particularly nonfiction writing, presumes some prior know-ledge. In fact it is generally accepted that prior knowledge is the best predictor of reading comprehension. Even an article as accessible (to experienced readers at least) as Grady's assumes a great deal. Does a student know what *chemotherapy* or *leukemia* are? If not, comprehen-sion breaks down early.

Kelly Gallagher has developed a practice called "Article of the Week" to help build this general world knowledge. He uses articles like Grady's to create an awareness of issues, terms, and positions that are being discussed in serious newspapers and magazines. Here he explains his strategy:

> *Part of the reason my students have such a hard time reading is because they bring little prior knowledge and background to the written page. They can decode the words, but the words remain meaningless without a foundation of knowledge.*

To help build my students' prior knowledge, I assign them an "Article of the Week" every Monday morning. By the end of the school year I want them to have read 35 to 40 articles about what is going on in the world. It is not enough to simply teach my students to recognize theme in a given novel; if my students are to become literate, they must broaden their reading experiences into real-world text. (n.d.)

A set of his most recent choices can be found on his website: http://kellygallagher.org/resources/articles.html

---

researcher with a knack for clarifying comparisons, particularly the framing metaphor of "reprogramming." And at the end she returns to the situation of the patient, given new life by this miraculous treatment:

> *When the fevers hit, he had no idea that might be a good sign. Instead, he assumed the treatment was not working. But a few weeks later, he said that his oncologist, Dr. Alison Loren, told him, "We can't find any cancer in your bone marrow."*
>
> *Remembering the moment, Mr. Ludwig paused and said, "I got goose bumps just telling you those words."*

"I feel wonderful," Mr. Ludwig said during a recent interview. "I walked 18 holes on the golf course this morning."

Building her story around the experience of this patient is not simply a tactic to keep people reading; Grady feels that she has the ethical obligation to show how scientific work plays out in the experience of patients. I will quote at length from an email on this issue that she sent me:

I also feel an ethical obligation to look for people—real live patients—when I'm writing about medicine. A new treatment may sound great, but what's it really like to go through it, to be the patient? Without that, the information is sterile, in a vacuum. I am writing about stuff that has a real impact on people's lives, so I try to capture some of that.

I went to a conference years ago where reporters and doctors were meeting to talk about the way medical information was reported to the public, and one of the doctors stood up and denounced us all for writing about patients and their experiences. He said those details were "anecdotal" and inherently biased and subjective. My immediate, emotional reaction was to roll my eyes and think he was in his ivory tower and out of touch with the real world if he thought people would be willing to wade through dry piles of bloodless data. That's the difference between a medical journal and a newspaper, I thought. I also thought it was his way of trying to control the message: leave those whining patients out of it. They don't know what's good for them. But I could also see his point: maybe thousands of people take a pill or have an operation, and I quote a handful. Are they representative? My only answer is, we do our best, try to use our judgment to find people who seem sane and rational and fair-minded. And I find that people who agree to be interviewed about their experiences as patients seem to rise to the occasion and try very hard to be fair and honest, because they like the idea of helping people who are in the same boat decide what to do.

In fact, Grady tells not one story, but several, shifting expertly among them. There is the story of the patient, the story of the research discovery, and the story of the treatment itself in which very technical information is made accessible through familiar story analogies. We are never far from narrative.

Sometimes the concept of metaphor is taught (or *mistaught*) as a "figure of speech"—which makes it seem nothing more than kind of fancy language. Yet the metaphor and its near cousins (simile, analogy, parable) are critical in helping us understand scientific processes, and they are closely tied to story. A term like *serial killers* in Grady's article connects the new (the engineered destruction of cancer cells) to the known (movies and news events we are familiar with). It evokes a well-known story type or, in psychological terms, a schema. Coming with it are key associations of ruthlessness, destructiveness, lack of selectivity, even brainwashing. Without this metaphoric assistance, we would lose ourselves in technical language.

Metaphors matter. One absolutely essential comprehension strategy is assigning significance (Keene and Zimmermann, 2007)—and writers cue us into what they feel is central (e.g., titles, repetitions). Locate the key metaphor a writer is using and you locate a key explanatory strategy—guaranteed. The more unfamiliar the topic (clearly the case in cancer research), the more essential.

In my experience metaphors are often hard-earned, and once discovered extremely valuable, as they connect the new to the known. Writers often make a big bet on them, and readers should too. Not only do metaphors enable comprehension, they can shape the scientific process itself. One of the most chilling sections in Siddhartha Mukherjee's award-winning study of cancer, *The Emperor of All Maladies* (2010), described a push for radical mastectomies—a term that still carries a load of terror. The term itself is derived from the Latin word *radix*—meaning "root"; *radish* has the same derivation. The conception was that cancer had to be uprooted with major excavating surgery; the deeper you went, the more likely that all the roots would be pulled up. One of the major proponents, William Steward Halstead, scorned the misplaced kindness that kept surgeons from stripping away major muscles for fear of disfiguring:

> Instead of stripping away the thin pectoralis minor, which had little function, Halstead decided to dig deeper into the breast cavity, cutting through the pectoralis major, the large prominent muscle responsible for moving the shoulder and hand. (Mukherjee, 64–65)

Later, he would also slice through the collar bone to clean out lymph nodes. Although some women survived and seemed cured, it later becomes evident that they were cured because their cancer was not widespread (at an early stage in common terminology). They would have been "cured" with much less invasive surgery. For those women whose cancer had spread, the surgery was ineffective. Mukherjee's major criticism of this group of surgeons was the way they became trapped in their own metaphor of "radicalism."

Picture Books as Stories of Information

When I would recreate myself, I seek the darkest wood, the thickest and most interminable, and to the citizen, most dismal swamp. I enter a swamp as a sacred place.

HENRY DAVID THOREAU, "WALKING"

Writers interested in conveying information have a choice between two primary structures—the list and the story. For example, in writing about crows one could list the primary features or topics to be addressed—mating, feeding, communication—and devote a section to each, as Laurence Pringle does in his excellent book, *Listen to the Crows*. Using this approach, an author writes of crows in general, using the plural—as Pringle does here:

> *Crows eat just about anything—insects, earthworms, snails, clams, mice, grain, carrion (dead animals). About 650 different kinds of food have been found in the stomachs of crows. Their diet changes with the seasons. Beetles are abundant in May and June so crows eat lots of beetles then. Later in the summer, they fill up with wild berries, crickets, and grasshoppers that are plentiful. (1976, 6)*

This is a clear and interesting example of what Nell Duke (2004) calls *non-narrative informational writing*. It is the staple of encyclopedias, Wikipedia, and textbooks. Yet, from the standpoint of sustained reading, this decision poses risks for the writer: the accumulation of information, at some point, may be hard to process, and the reader seeks the relief of a less dense form—not surprisingly narrative. Pringle leavens his book with italicized narrative sections:

> *Listen to the crows. Three baby crows are in their nest, high in the tree. It is a big sturdy nest, made of sticks and lined with softer material such as grasses, moss, and deer hair. The little crows are hungry. They give hoarse little caws. Then a parent flies into sight and a great chorus of high pitched cries come from young crows. (18)*

Passages like this also particularize the topic: Pringle identified specific crows and not simply crows in general. For the young (and not so young) readers, this strategy creates a feeling of empathy that the more categorical information cannot create.

The Walk. The walk is a staple of nonfiction writing, a loose temporal form adored by essay writers like Virginia Woolf, Annie Dillard, William Hazlitt, and, of course, Henry David Thoreau. It provides a loose personal narrative thread to link observations to. Naturalists are invariably walkers. My father clearly was. Every day in the summer he would strap on his World War II knapsack, call to our dachshund Hans, and head for a wooded area near our house to look for insects that preyed on mosquitoes. Around Christmas time he would head off with binoculars and dog for the Audubon bird count. Being a scientist, in my mind, was always closely tied to walking.

Not surprisingly the excursion becomes the vehicle for many children's informational books; the little boy or girl (or even the animal) sets off from home and makes discoveries or faces challenges in the natural world. The excursion provides a temporal, personal thread to connect information to. And because it is presented as a singular instance, it invites identification in a way that general information (about polar bears, for example), might not. It has the immediacy of the story. The excursion form also allows the writer and reader the chance to move freely since there is often no traditional plot—so it might be seen as a hybrid of the list and the story. The form also allows the information to be bound by a unit of time, often a day, which gives it the form that students often use in their own writing, their bed-to-bed stories.

Box Turtle at Long Pond by William George is a good example. It begins with the beginning of the day:

> *It is dawn at Long Pond. The white mist covers the water. Little warblers awaken and fly from the tall pine trees to blueberry bushes below. They dart to the pond's edge and take long sips of water.* (1989)

As dawn breaks the box turtle begins to stir and he makes his way to the pond. And so begins a series of encounters—with a chipmunk, with earthworms that emerge after a storm, with a raccoon that forces the turtle to close its shell, with grasshoppers, and a grouse, until the day ends:

The sun sets on the side of Long Pond. The evening air grows cooler. The box turtle burrows in the soft pine needles to stay warm, and closes its eyes. It has been a long day. (1989)

The frame of a day is also used by Sarah Marwil Lamstein in her lovely book *Big Night for Salamanders* (2010) which is framed by the day in early spring when spotted salamanders leave their winter burrows and migrate to vernal pools to mate.

This excursion pattern is also employed by Eric Carle in his well-known *A House for Hermit Crab*, but here the time frame is a year with hermit crab accumulating friends (anemones, starfish, lantern fish) until he must change shells at the end of the year—and it thinks about new accumulations ("Barnacles! Clown Fish? Sand dollars! Electric eels!"). Interestingly both Carle and Lamstein supplement their excursion narratives with more conventional glossaries and background information that one assumes will be embedded in the oral reading. So they mix what I would call categorical information and narrative information. In fact, some nonfiction authors have told me that the standards for documentation and historical accuracy are higher than they have been in the past.

These children's writers also have a sense of what I call the "romance of information"—that is, they have a knack for the odd and surprising fact (e.g., blood resembles seawater or crows eat 650 different kinds of plants and animals) that will stay with a reader. Take *Polar Bears* by Sandra Markle (2004) where you can learn that a polar bear can swim sixty miles without stopping, can smell prey twenty miles away; and with a little calculating you can figure out that a mature polar bear can hold one hundred pounds in its stomach. Add in photographs of the blood-soaked muzzle of a polar bear eating a beluga whale and the book is irresistible and memorable. Markle knows her audience.

The great children's science writer, Seymour Simon, is a master of the surprising fact. Take this stunning opening to his book, *The Heart: Our Circulatory System*:

Make a fist. This is the size of your heart. (1996)

The heart, he informs his readers, weighs as much as a sneaker. He asks his readers to imagine the work of the heart with this unforgettable comparison:

Try squeezing a rubber ball with your hand. Squeeze it hard once a second. You hand will get tired in a minute or two. Yet your heart beats every second of every day. (1996)

Informative. Yes. But writing like this is surprising, arresting; we almost feel a bodily jolt of energy—and a sense of awe.

The excursion frame, with a child leaving the confines of a home to witness a natural process, also has ethical dimensions. Writers are doing more than conveying facts or information—they are portraying a stance toward nature itself, an "environmental imagination" (Buell 1995). By creating a character, similar in age to the reader, who makes the excursion, they show what it is like to assume the role of the naturalist; or as Buell would argue, they fulfill a major criterion of an environmental text: "Human accountability to the environment is part of the text's ethical orientation" (7).

This accountability has at least two parts; the obligation to witness and the responsibility of stewardship. In *Big Night for Salamanders* (Lamstein 2010), the young boy, Evan, is present, with a flashlight, to witness the migration and the illustrations convey a sense of wonder and reverence. He also works to enable the salamanders to cross a road safely, creating a sign that he illuminates with a flashlight, "Go Slow Salamander Crossing." Pure "information" would lack this illustration of ethical purpose.

Medical Detectives—Information as Drama

When I was thinking of examples of the science writing I like best, I immediately thought of the "Annals of Medicine" column that has been a feature of *The New Yorker* for decades. I loved the way these great writers would embed scientific knowledge within a narrative of mystery and detection. One particular example that stayed vividly in my memory concerned the *Helicobacter* bacteria (see Figure 6.1), which is now known to cause ulcers, stomach cancer, and perhaps even chronic indigestion. Yet in the early 1980s, no reputable scientist thought any bacteria could survive in the cauldron of the stomach, where digestive enzymes and stomach acid worked to kill microbes in food. The accepted scientific position was that, so far as bacteria were concerned, the stomach was "sterile."

The New Yorker writer Terence Monmaney (1993) tells the story of how this scientific consensus was overturned by an iconoclastic young

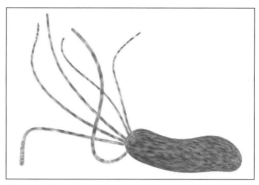

Figure 6.1 *Helicobacter* Bacteria

Australian researcher who proved the scientific community wrong. Up until his work, the accepted view on ulcers was that they were caused by stress; the accepted treatment was a costly long-term maintenance regimen of drugs like Zantac—and lifestyle changes to reduce stress.

As Monmaney tells the story, Barry Marshall, a thirty-two-year-old resident in internal medicine in Perth, believed that ulcers were caused by a bacteria that he had identified in almost all the patients he treated for ulcers. But the presence of the bacteria, though surprising, was not evidence of cause; it could be a co-occurrence. To complicate matters, when he had laboratory pigs and rats ingest the bacteria, they did not develop ulcers (but when you consider what rats and pigs normally eat, perhaps they easily resist the bug).

So he became his own test case.

Without any permission from his hospital (it would surely have been refused), he drank about a billion of these bacteria and waited to see what would happen. For a week, he experienced nothing more than a grumbling stomach, but around the eighth day, he began having headaches, his breath smelled foul, he was irritable and hoarse. Around the tenth day, an endoscopy showed his stomach lining, which was totally healthy at the beginning of the test, to be inflamed, with "swarms of bacteria seeming to hover around inflamed stomach cells" (66). Although he was able to fight off progression to a full-blown ulcer, he had proved his point. The bacteria could survive—even thrive—in the stomach and cause damage to the stomach wall.

Now many ulcers are "cured" by a short, and inexpensive, antibiotic treatment—saving billions of dollars. Marshall even speculated that this bacteria could be a cause of stomach cancer, the second most common form of cancer worldwide (behind only lung cancer), which also has subsequently been shown to be true. So the *Helicobacter* bacteria went from being an incidental and insignificant stomach bacteria to "arguably the commonest chronic bacterial infection in man."

One of Monmaney's big challenges is to explain *how* the bacteria actually does survive in the inhospitable stomach. He does it with the metaphoric flair of a great teacher:

> *Once* Helicobacter *reaches the stomach, it probably does not linger in the open cavity—a tossing sea of toxic chemicals. It heads for cover. The bacterium's helical shape seems to have been designed for speedy travel in a dense medium.* Helicobacter *is living torque; a microscopic Roto-Rooter, it corkscrews through the mucus. Then, instead of penetrating the cells of the stomach lining, it settles in the mucus just beyond the lining. More often than not it settles in the pylorus [the base of the stomach]. No one knows why. Under the microscope, a* Helicobacter *looks like a satellite image of an armada gathered off a ragged shore. At the end of the bacterium is a cluster of long, wispy, curving flagella, which may serve as anchors. It's a graceful menace.* (1993, 69)

By using a set of nautical images (armada, shore, anchor, and even the image of the corkscrew—evoking a submarine), we can visualize the opportunistic movement of *Helicobacter*. The bacterium also has an evolutionary adaptation that provides a vital defense:

> *It's coat is studded with enzymes that converts urea—a waste product, virtually unlimited supplies of which can be found in the stomach—directly into carbon dioxide and also into ammonia, a strong alkali. Thus* Helicobacter *ensconces itself in an acid neutralizing mist. In like fashion, it generates another antacid—bicarbonate, as in Alka-Seltzer.* (69)

How wonderful that the bacteria can construct its own Alka-Seltzer-like cloud to protect itself. Could anything be clearer? Monmaney takes us through the science, connecting the new to the familiar, so that we feel smart—I get it.

The Romance of Science

We are all familiar with the image of scientists as dispassionate, objective, scrupulous—you know, not swayed by emotion. It's the way they sometimes appear in their more formal writing. But get them talking about their work and they are as passionate as dancers or artists or Patriots fans. In my own class, I invited my colleague Rob Drugan to come to class to talk about the research on stress and resilience in rats—in preparation we had read one of his papers on his experiments. We had all struggled with terms like *endogenous*, referring to the capacity of stressed rats to essentially self-medicate. Language like this:

> *This pattern suggested that resilience might involve activation of an endogenous benzodiazepine-like compound, possibly an allostatic modulator of the $GABA_A$ receptor like allopregnanolone. From the ISS model, we have observed in resilient rats protection from stressor-induced glucocorticoid increases and immune activation.* (Drugan et al., 2013)

Talk about text complexity! *But*, when Rob came through the door he was nothing like his written self. He began by announcing the results of a new experiment, and he promised us that the results would "blow our socks off."

And he was right.

He described his work with a swim test during which rats would emit a high-pitched shriek, inaudible to the human ear, that he showed correlated with ability to cope with stress—and this test would dramatically improve techniques for identifying resilient rats. He speculated that this shriek was probably some kind of warning that only the most resilient rats would emit. His work represented a step forward in determining why some animals (including humans) can be in stressful situations and not develop major stress disabilities but others do. For example, some soldiers develop posttraumatic stress disorder from combat situations and others, in the same circumstances, do not. What internal mechanism might explain the difference? Rob speculated there is an "endogenous" mechanism, the release of a valium-like chemical, that for some rats mitigates the stress and makes them resilient. The word made sense now.

Obviously much of this work is technical and decidedly unromantic, but I suspect scientists like my colleague can trace their fascination to a person, book, or experience that revealed the process of discovery. Michelle Nijhuis, a writer for *National Geographic* and *Smithsonian*, makes this claim:

> *Science writing has a reputation for bloodlessness, but in many ways it is the most human of disciplines. Science, after all, is a quest, and as such it's one of the oldest and most enduring stories we have. It's about searching for answers, struggling with setbacks, persevering through tedium and competing with colleagues all eager to put forth their own ideas about how the world works.* (2013)

A book that stands out for me was Paul De Kruif's 1926 classic, *Microbe Hunters*, a series of portraits of scientists who discovered the microorganisms that caused disease and helped develop vaccines to prevent them. I read it at about the time when polio was being conquered by the Salk vaccine—I recall standing in lines, stretching hundreds of yards, at our elementary school to get the shot. We would not have to spend time in the "iron lungs" like some of those in our town who were born too early. So the book had very personal relevance to me.

Microbe Hunters is florid, and dramatic, and personal, as in this description of Louis Pasteur discovering small organisms (and no yeast globules) in nonfermenting "wine," a situation that was plaguing France at the time.

> *No yeast globules here, no, but something different, something strange that he had not seen before, great tangled dancing masses of rod-like things, some of them alone, some drifting along like strings of boats, all of them shimmying with weird incessant vibration. He hardly dared to guess at their size—they were much smaller than the yeasts—they were only one-twenty-five-thousandth of an inch long.* (62)

He had, of course, discovered microorganisms. De Kruif was masterful, though rarely subtle, in conveying Pasteur's persistence, his obsessive fascination, and the extraordinary excitement of scientific discovery. What young reader wants subtlety, after all?

I recently discovered that I shared the experience with others of my generation, including Joan Ehrenfeld, a noted ecologist at Rutgers University, who writes about the factors that influenced her to become a biologist. A major influence was her mother, actually a violinist and music teacher, who "valued, above everything, the creative use of the mind to explore, learn, and find new ways of looking at old things."

Science epitomized those values completely. So I suppose it was not surprising that as a child, I took books out of the library about science and scientists; Paul de Kruif's "Microbe Hunters" was one of my early favorites. In the 1950's, as a girl in a Queens, NY public school, this was a bit weird, for sure. But that book was inspiring, and I vividly remember being unable to put it down or stop thinking about the scientific heroes that it described. Shortly after that, Sputnik went up, and the world changed. The call went out for American students to study science, and this message permeated society. I can remember standing around the playground of my elementary school, talking with my classmates about it, and discussing how we might become scientists as a result. (2012)

At a time when there is concern about recruiting students into the sciences, we all can help by connecting them to great science writing, which is rarely found in textbooks. We need to reveal to students, not simply the names and labels, but the process of scientific work, the spirit, the itch, the obsession, even the beauty. It is writing about action, filled with mutation, transformation, attack and defense, extinction and survival, puzzlement and discovery.

Nothing is still, not even for Eric Carle's hermit crab, who starts his journey with: "Time to move."

PART 3

STORIES
WHERE YOU
LEAST EXPECT
THEM

INTUITIVE,
REASONING, REFLECTIVE,
FACULTIES.

LITERARY,
OBSERVING, KNOWING,
FACULTIES.

quality

discovery

reading

CAN AN ARGUMENT BE A STORY?

CH 7

Stories are how we understand the interrelationship of events. Stories are at the heart of how we learn because they create memories and provide details we want to know. Stories grab us in a way no list of facts could ever do.

JIM McELHANEY, LEGENDARY LITIGATOR AND COLUMNIST
FOR THE *ABA JOURNAL*

A few years ago, the inevitable happened and I was picked for jury duty. I was usually bounced during jury selection, but I was selected for one trial. I had a week to watch lawyers at work on a case of aggravated drunk driving. The bare details of the case were these: a young man was seen driving a van with a young woman in the passenger's seat. He passed a local policeman who recognized him and knew his license was suspended. So he put on the light bar on top of his cruiser and followed the van.

That much was established. When the van stopped, the officer claimed that he saw the passengers switching seats because when he got to the door, the young man was in the passenger seat. According to this man's version, he'd been there the whole time and the young woman was, in effect, a designated driver (and maybe something more). Since the defendant had a suspended license, this was a crucial fact.

As jurors, we had not left the world of story—we were locked in it. Which of these versions was more plausible? We were taken to the van to look at the configuration of the front seats with a console with cup holders between them. We checked out the view the policeman would have had from the rear of the van; we heard from the woman who swore that she was the one driving. The defendant's very able lawyer argued that it was physically impossible to make such a passenger switch over the console so quickly—yet the policeman, under intense questioning, didn't budge in his claim that they did a switcheroo.

Our job was to sort out these stories. In the jury room, there was a sense of relief that we could finally talk about what we had been hearing. The foreman raised the question of the passenger switch—could it have been done as the policeman claimed? One juror said, "Sure, we had a van like that and we did it all the time on long trips when we wanted to switch drivers without stopping. It's not hard." Apparently, it's a common practice because a couple of other jurors told the same stories, sometimes demonstrating how it could be done.

And that was not the end of the stories. According to New Hampshire law, we could look at the defendant's criminal record, in his case, pages and pages of violations for drinking and driving. As we passed it around, we could imagine his life as an uncontrollable drinker, an alcoholic, who could not be stopped by any threat of imprisonment—he was so deep into violation that a conviction would result in a mandatory year in prison.

We voted to convict, and I distinctly recall our filing back into the courtroom where the defendant sat at his table with his lawyer. They say you can tell a verdict by just looking at the faces of jurors, and I can believe it. I know I was projecting the story forward. He would enter the county prison, adjacent to the courthouse, for a year. We had taken that time from him.

In the courtroom, as my story of jury duty indicates, much of the contest was about which version of the story made the most sense. As a jury we tested these versions against our own personal histories; story bumped up against story. This is the nature of judicial or forensic rhetoric—to assign responsibility by establishing the nature of past action. When I raised this issue with a Superior Court judge in our district, he agreed that storytelling is an absolutely crucial skill for lawyers. "I remember arguing a case for a defendant in a wrongful termination case. I told the story of his work for that company, actually his last day, and finished, 'And they discarded him like the morning trash!'" He added that he won the case.

Arguments and Narratives

In his classic text on the aims of discourse, James Kinneavy (1971) defines four broad purposes for using language—to persuade (e.g., a political speech), to entertain (a short story), to inform (an encyclopedia entry), and to express (a diary). There is, of course, huge overlap, but Kinneavy claims that in most cases there is one predominating aim. Narrative is clearly the backbone of three of these aims. There is no need to really argue that narrative is central to literary enjoyment, or that it is the primary way we express ourselves in informal speech or writing (i.e., expressive discourse), for example, when we are recounting our day to a friend or spouse.

In the previous chapters, I have made the case that science writing invariably involves processes of change that makes narrative the natural form for communication and indeed that we rely on narrative structures for comprehension.

The narrative roots of persuasive discourse are less obvious. And writers of the Common Core have been quick to contrast narrative with the supposedly more mature and functional forms of argument. Steve Zemelman comments: "The standards drafters continue to denigrate narrative when they give talks, suggesting it's a frill, a concession to young people's immature preoccupation with their own lives" (2011). Even CCSS documents typically spend a great deal of time telling the *story* of how they were created to establish credibility.

To be fair, this dividing line has long been common in reading and writing instruction. Typically, argument and narrative are seen as distinct—one relying on claims and evidence, the other on chronology and the unfolding of a conflict involving characters. Its tools are scene, detail, plot. The implicit, and at times explicit, message from the creators of the standards is this: in college and the workplace, we make arguments using evidence—we don't tell stories.

Yet argument is entwined with narrative. Judicial rhetoric, like the example I cited at the beginning of this chapter, is one of the three categories of arguments that Aristotle defined in his rhetoric—and it regularly involved contesting narratives. A second is ceremonial persuasion—the orations of funerals, graduations, letters of recommendation. It is rhetoric that focuses on praise and blame, giving meaning to the past. It is naturally rich in examples and stories: memorial services and wedding toasts, for example, are all about stories.

The third branch described by Aristotle is deliberative rhetoric, persuading an audience to take (or not take) an action; it is the rhetoric of policy making. Many public arguments involve problems that need to be acted upon. And all involve some form of narrative. Some problem demands attention (the cost of health care, overcrowding in a local school). To solve that problem, a body needs to construct a causal narrative about how this situation came about—and the role of argument is usually to construct the most plausible narrative, the one that gets cause-effect right. So any act of deliberation involves the question: "How did we get to this point?"

The other obvious question is "What do we do about it?" And here again this activity involves a narrative, or several narratives. Any action, if it is at all thoughtful, requires a prediction or projection. If we do x, will it solve the problem? Will it affect anyone negatively, provoking political resistance? Will it have unintended consequences? Predictions like this are another form of narrative, though ones that have to be imagined. It involves creating multiple scenarios, stories. What will be the probable outcome of any action taken?

Any decision maker acts within time, poised between past and future. Evidence and argument are crucial in establishing the most plausible story. But any attempt to separate narrative and argument, evidence and story, is seriously flawed, ignoring the time-bound (and emotional) nature of human decisions.

High School All Over Again

Life beyond school walls is not a particularly logical place. Kurt Vonnegut once mused that in high school, life revolved around popularity, cheerleaders, and football. Then he went to college and there were discussions about big issues and life philosophies. But after that, in the "real world," it was "high school all over again."

His observation comes to mind as I read the repeated conflation of "college ready" and "career ready" in the Common Core State Standards—as if these were the same thing, as if there was no gap between academic argumentation (the focus in the standards) and the way persuasion operates in the commercial and civic life where, in my view, narrative is paramount, as evidenced by books like Jonah Sachs' *Winning the Story Wars: Why Those Who Tell (and Live) the Best Stories Will Rule the Future* (2012); Annette Simmons' *Whoever Tells the Best Story Wins: How to Use Your Own Stories to Communicate with Power and Impact* (2007); Robert Dickman and Richard

Maxwell's *The Elements of Persuasion: Use Storytelling to Pitch Better, Sell Faster & Win More Business* (2007); Stephen Denning's *The Leader's Guide to Storytelling: Mastering the Art and Discipline of Business Narrative* (2011); and Peter Gruber's *Tell to Win: Connect, Persuade, and Triumph with the Hidden Power of Story* (2011).

We can start with a key definition of argument in the standards in which "argumentation" is distinguished from "persuasion," which I will quote in its entirety:

> *When writing to persuade, writers employ a variety of persuasive strategies. One common strategy is an appeal to the credibility, character, or authority of the writer (or speaker). When writers establish that they are knowledgeable or trustworthy, audiences are more likely to believe what they say. Another is the appeal to the audience's self-interest, sense of identity, or emotions, any of which can sway an audience. A logical argument, on the other hand, convinces the audience because of the perceived merit and reasonableness of the claims and proofs offered, rather than either the emotions the writing evokes in the audience or the character or credentials of the writer. The Standards place special emphasis on writing logical arguments as a particularly important form of college and career-ready writing.* (National Governors Association Center for Best Practices and Council of Chief State School Officers 2010c, 24)

This distinction of "argument" from "persuasion" has drawn little attention and to my knowledge no criticism.

Yet classical rhetoricians would surely balk at this choosing of appeals. They would see each as crucial in creating what Wayne Booth (1961) calls a "rhetorical stance"—a constructive balance of appeals. (He labels the

THE ETHICIST—STORIES THAT INVITE ARGUMENT

One of my favorite columns is the "Ethicist" section of *The New York Times Magazine.* The columnist, now Chuck Klosterman, responds to letters that describe ethical dilemmas with no clear and moral solution. Here is one of my favorites involving an Oreo "theft" from a minibar in a hotel. Here is the question:

> When I checked into a hotel in California, I was starving, so I ate the $6 box of Oreos from the minibar. Later that day, I walked down the street to a convenience store, bought an identical box for $2.50, and replenished the minibar before the hotel had a chance to restock it.
>
> Was this proper? My view is "no harm, no foul." In fact, my box was fresher: the Oreos I ate were going to expire three months before the box I replaced them with. (2010, mm22)

I present students with this question and have them freewrite their response. They usually agree with the writer, that since nothing substantially has changed, no wrong has been done. But a few are not so sure—hasn't he taken a service (the ready availability of Oreos) from the hotel—and not paid for it? How is this different from theft? Would you do this if you knew the owner of the hotel? If the act is "moral," why would it matter? What would happen if everyone felt at liberty to do this?

As a side note, this practice has apparently become so widespread that some hotels are placing a barcode on items so that they are charged to the room when they are removed. And the cost for this preventive measure is spread to all guests.

overreliance on logic as "the pedant's stance," a characteristic of some academic writing, actually bad academic writing.) The character of the speaker/writer is absolutely crucial—unless this person is trusted, no logical appeal will have much force. And as I argued earlier, this "persona" or guide is crucial in sustaining a reading—we will be spending time with this person(a). Likewise, any argument that fails to appeal to the emotions, values, hopes, fears, self-interest, or identity of an audience is doomed to fail. Indeed, the concept of "reasonableness," itself, involves our judgment on how these are addressed.

The Limits of Data

Marriage, she felt, was a fine arrangement generally, except one never got it generally. One got it very, very, specifically.

LORRIE MOORE, "REAL ESTATE"

I recently heard a curriculum director explain the changes in assessment this way: "In the past we relied on observation and anecdotes. Now we look to data." She clearly saw this as an advance. To rely on stories is to be unscientific, sentimental, impressionist, softheaded. Data are solid, objective. Which brings me to another story.

An all-too-familiar scenario. The tests are in, and it's cancer, uterine cancer—my wife and I are assured that it is a good one to get if you have to have cancer, relatively unlikely to spread. We sit in a consultation room with a cancer specialist from Mass General Hospital who makes weekly trips to Dover, New Hampshire, saving local patients the difficult trip into Boston. And he lays out the odds, 30% chance of reoccurrence with just radiation, 10% with radiation and chemo—what happens if we do nothing? (don't ask).

We get the numbers and probabilities, as we should, but my wife finds them unsatisfactory, cold, distant. She asks later, "How do I know where I fit into those numbers?" After the consultation she talks with others who have gone through the kind of treatment proposed, how they dealt with it, how they thought about it and the cloud of reoccurrence that hangs over them. She needed stories, testimony. And she appreciated the sharing that seems to naturally occur when you join this club.

We have an ambivalent attitude toward hard statistical data; our rational side tells us that this kind of evidence should be conclusive and should trump anecdotal accounts that may well be unrepresentative, and, given the fallibility of human memory, not all that accurate. Yet we are rarely persuaded by numerical data alone. Joseph Stalin is credited with the comment: "If only one man dies of hunger, that is a tragedy. If millions die, that's only statistics." Well, he should know.

We simply cannot translate bare numbers into recognizable human reality; our eyes glaze over. They don't activate or develop what Robert

ACTIVIST MARSHALL GANZ ON LEADERSHIP AND STORYTELLING

A leadership story is first a story of self, a story of why I've been called. Some people say, "I don't want to talk about myself," but if you don't interpret to others your calling and your reason for doing what you're doing, do you think it will just stay uninterpreted? No. Others will interpret if for you. You don't have a choice if you want to be a leader. You have to claim authorship of your story and learn to tell it to others so they can understand the values that move you to act, because it might move them as well.

Coles calls "the moral imagination." I believe the same process is occurring in schools where teachers are now coached to rely on "data," often test scores, aggregated, disconnected from individual children. Teachers' resistance comes from the same difficulty my wife had—where am I (and my students) in these numbers?

Put another way, we may piously claim that "all human life is sacred," but we rarely act that way. We care more, feel more, about those in our group, with people who share some identity. Arguments based primarily on statistics typically fail because we feel that these numbers refer to "others," and may even come from others. These "facts" fail to penetrate the group affiliation that shapes our beliefs—and even more so, our actions. We have a predisposition to ration our empathy, to limit it to self, then family, tribe, and only with real effort beyond.

According to Timothy Wilson, author of *Redirect: The Surprising New Science of Psychological Change* (2011), stories are more powerful than data because they allow individuals to identify emotionally with people they might otherwise see as outsiders. Emotional and powerful storytelling can affect our moral sensibilities, altering the boundaries between "us" and "them." They can change us in a way that pure numbers cannot. One of the great moral voices today is *The New York Times* columnist Nicholas Kristof, who has exposed the hideous trade in young women sold as sex slaves. His gift is to be specific, personal, so that we imagine these women as our daughters, our sisters, how we can imagine their degradation and destroyed lives.

> *Anyone who thinks it is hyperbole to describe sex trafficking as slavery should look at the maimed face of a teenage girl, Long Pross.*
>
> *Glance at Pross from her left, and she looks like a normal, fun-loving girl, with a pretty face and a joyous smile. Then move around, and you see where her brothel owner gouged out her right eye.* (2009)

Sheer numbers cannot accomplish this.

This claim for the moral power of storytelling is so widely accepted by those investigating human change and persuasion that we need to question any reductive focus on rational argumentation—that is, if we are interested in professional, civic, and commercial persuasion *as it really happens*.

It is gratifying to see young writers learning the narrative skills that make them effective persuaders. The standard advice to students is to get their thesis stated in the first paragraph. But actual writers (and readers) are rarely that impatient. Rather, the writer builds to a thesis, often beginning with narrative to create tension and emotional interest in the topic. This eighth-grade writer does exactly that, letting her title ("Too Young to Race") provide enough focus at the beginning.

> *I watched in horror as Eight Belles, a three-year-old filly racing in the Kentucky Derby, collapsed to the dirt track. Her fluid stride harshly ceased as her muscular chest, and then her smooth dark head, hit the ground. She had just galloped away, full of grace and athleticism, from finishing second in the mile and one quarter mile horse race. My heart pounded as equine ambulances and nervous people surrounded the fallen horse, speaking brusquely into walkie-talkies and pacing back and forth. She had broken her two front ankles while running and could no longer support her own weight. The veterinarians made the decision—she had to be euthanized.* (Katherine Engalichev)

This opening affects us emotionally in a way that statistics (which she uses later) cannot.

Rita Charon makes the same point in her deeply moving book *Narrative Medicine* in which she sees a primary place for narrative in the way doctors understand the experience of patients, an act she calls "bearing witness." Stories build a relationship that can be the foundation of treatment. She describes her own practice where she will begin a patient history with the invitation: "I will be your doctor, so I have to learn a great deal about your body and your health and your life. Please tell me what I should know about your situation." And then she listens:

I do my best to not say a word, to not write in the medical chart, but to absorb all that he [a forty-six-year-old Dominican man with possible heart problems] emits about himself—about his health concerns, his family, his work, his fears, and his hopes. I listen not only for the content of his narrative but also for its form—its temporal course, its images, its associated subplots, its silences, where he chooses to begin in telling about himself, and how he sequences symptoms with other life events. After a few minutes the patient stops talking and begins to weep. I ask him why he cries. He says, "No one ever let me do this before." (2006, 177)

Charon claims that this sustained attention to patient narratives can work against the short-circuiting movement from test results to diagnosis. This narrative attention builds empathy and trust, a good investment of time.

Making "sound" arguments is crucially important, but they rarely can carry the day unless they both employ narratives and embed evidence in broader stories that fully engage listeners. Or as Emmy-winning NBC reporter Kare Anderson claims: "Whoever most vividly characterizes a situation usually determines how others view it, discuss it and make decisions about it" (2012).

Tastes Like Sprite to Me

We can put the Common Core claims about argument to a test by looking at a company whose business is persuasion. We can take as a case the work of Lippincott, an international branding company. Lippincott was founded in 1943, and in 1946 created the iconic Campbell soup label that Andy Warhol made famous. In the early '60s, Lippincott helped introduce a lemony, carbonated drink to compete with 7UP and named it Sprite. Lippincott's clients include some of the largest and best-known companies in the world—Samsung, Walmart, Dell, McDonalds, Starbucks. If we are looking at "real-world" persuasion, Lippincott marketing employees have much to teach us—and because they must articulate their approach to clients, they have to be specific about how they view persuasion in a hyper-interconnected age.

A revealing internal document, "Building Winning Brands in a Radically Transparent World," begins with this striking observation:

The way people interact with brands has changed dramatically over the past decade. The rapid rise of hyper-connected consumers—enabled by new technologies—has shifted the power balance. Customers now have the upper hand, with ready access to the truth about brands. It is a radically transparent world where customers are in control. (n.d., 2)

In other words, Speedo can make claims about its swim goggles, but I can also read dozens of online user accounts that evaluate performance. But hyper-connected companies can help shape this perception. Lippincott believes that the key to this effective self-advocacy is to create authentic stories—"real stories, with emotional resonance. Stories that help people identify with the real character of the brand. Stories that crucially are based on core truth and stand the test of experience." These stories are "fundamentally a journey that uses *traditional narrative devices of goal, conflict, and hero* to powerfully express a theme that engages and motivates its audiences"(n.d.) (emphasis added).

In Lippincott's view, a brand story is a tool to engage, inspire, and galvanize key audiences (sometimes customers, but often employees) around a shared purpose and in alignment with corporate strategy. It humanizes the company as a way for organizations that often lack humanity (e.g., big corporations) to form more intimate and personal connections with stakeholders, allowing them to hook into the narratives of others as a way of building and strengthening those connections.

In constructing a brand story, a company employs its strengths and history as proof points for a narrative arc that supports the corporate vision and business strategy. It can be a way to recast negative elements of a company's history—a bankruptcy, say, or product recall—into obstacles that the company/hero must overcome to progress along its journey. A brand story also puts forward a goal that's bigger than just making money; this goal elevates what it means to be a customer or an employee beyond the everyday realities of buying and selling to something vital and exciting. The brand story also helps to articulate the character of an organization, in the same way that the actions of a protagonist in a novel serve to demonstrate his or her personality. And like many good stories, there's room for a sequel, so the brand story can adapt and change over time without being in conflict with its past story.

So, although the creators of the CCSS may claim that we should move beyond narratives in the workplace—this Park Avenue company would disagree.

The Gettysburg Address—Lincoln's Great Story

Even if we shift to the kinds of nonfiction documents stressed in the CCSS, narrative is more evident than you might expect. In an earlier chapter, I suggested, fairly breezily, that the best advice for readers of nonfiction was to read as if it is a story. Suppose we take this advice and apply it to a piece of nonfiction, say, the most famous speech in American history, as if it is a story.

GETTYSBURG ADDRESS

Four score and seven years ago our fathers brought forth on this continent, a new nation, conceived in Liberty, and dedicated to the proposition that all men are created equal.

Now we are engaged in a great civil war, testing whether that nation, or any nation so conceived and so dedicated, can long endure. We are met on a great battle-field of that war. We have come to dedicate a portion of that field, as a final resting place for those who here gave their lives that that nation might live. It is altogether fitting and proper that we should do this.

But, in a larger sense, we can not dedicate—we can not consecrate—we can not hallow—this ground. The brave men, living and dead, who struggled here, have consecrated it, far above our poor power to add or detract. The world will little note, nor long remember what we say here, but it can never forget what they did here. It is for us the living, rather, to be dedicated here to the unfinished work which they who fought here have thus far so nobly advanced. It is rather for us to be here dedicated to the great task remaining before us—that from these honored dead we take increased devotion to that cause for which they gave the last full measure of devotion—that we here highly resolve that these dead shall not have died in vain—that this nation, under God, shall have a new birth of freedom—and that government of the people, by the people, for the people, shall not perish from the earth.

I would contend that this speech makes more sense *as a narrative* than as a traditional argument with assertions and evidence. Lincoln creates a national narrative to define the significance of what happened in the battle; the tenses in the speech change from past, to present, to future—beginning with the defining document, The Declaration of Independence, and its claims about equality. It is the Declaration, written "four score and seven years ago," that begins the story of American identity.

As Gary Wills notes in *Lincoln at Gettysburg* (2006), Lincoln bypasses the Constitution, which makes no claim for human equality; it allowed slavery to persist and even counts Negroes as three-fifths of a person for census purposes. It is a provisional step toward realizing the anchoring principles of the United States.

Moving forward toward the present, the battle itself is viewed as a test to see if the values in the Declaration can prevail, if a nation can endure remaining faithful to them. The final part of the speech shifts to the future, and to the responsibility of his audience to take on "the great task remaining before us," to dedicate themselves (ourselves) to fulfilling the ideals of the Declaration. There is "unfinished business" to be accomplished. If the Declaration was a first birth of freedom, the heroic acts of Union soldiers creates the possibility for a "new birth." As Wills argues, Lincoln changed the historical narrative and the rationale for the war, locating it as an extension—and test—of the moral values in the Declaration.

To repeat, arguments often take narrative form because all important decisions and debates are located in time. Key events precede any act of rhetoric; indeed, they create the need for speaking (or writing); they provoke it. Something has happened (or not happened), something has been said (or not said), some problem is unmet, some calamity has occurred. There is then a case to be made for a kind of response—a plan of action, a new understanding of the situation, a challenge to accepted wisdom. Then, often, there is a look to the future—"so what"—what advantage do we gain by this change, this proposal, this alteration (often a place for appeals to emotion, hope, vision)? Where do we go from here? As I state it here, it sounds formulaic—but in great speeches, like the one Martin Luther King gave just before his assassination, "The Mountaintop Speech," it can be profoundly uplifting. It follows the arc of human desire.

The Inescapable Need for Plot

It may seem that I am evading the issue—the examples I have given to this point are not the "arguments" with claims and evidence that the CCSS claim are crucial for college and career. It seems obvious and self-evident that rational arguments take a nonnarrative form, centering on the logical support of claims. Examples from branding companies and famous speeches do not obviate that fact.

I realize that I can be accused of still languishing in the land of creative nonfiction, addicted to literary examples, and not the prose of "the real world." To that I plead guilty, but would be hard-pressed to locate writers of extended, widely read arguments that don't do something similarly literary—Michael Pollan, Stephen Johnson, David Brooks, Thomas Friedman, Barbara Ehrenreich, Anul Gawande, Jeffrey Toobin are all examples. The widely viewed TED talks are filled with deftly crafted stories.

Yet a far less widely read genre, call it the academic essay or research report, would seem to be an exception. Perhaps in these we truly pass out of storyland, into a timeless realm of logic, of assertion and evidence.

Or perhaps not.

To repeat: all arguments exist in time. They are responsive to some prior events or prior discourse. In any academic field, there is a body of scholarship that precedes our contribution (if there is no body, there is no field). There is a context, the conversation has been going on, and an academic writer needs to fit his or her work into it—assertions and claims cannot be made in a vacuum. This positioning of one's argument is hard and important narrative work. Inexperienced academics frequently bungle this context-building; they treat it as a call to simply list relevant reading, as if to show they have done their homework, a fatal misunderstanding of the work that is needed.

When done well, this "introduction" is a story of some line of inquiry that establishes the necessity of the writer's project. There is something unresolved: there are contradictory interpretations, a gap in knowledge, new critical perspectives to be employed, new evidence to be explained, new tools that can provide new data. There is trouble. When done well, one feels a sense of necessity, even inevitability, as if prior work is leading, inexorably, to the writer's project. It promises to make a contribution; something critical is at stake. To the outsider even these skilled entries may seem "academic," but to insiders they can generate intellectual excitement, or, when done poorly, they are perceived as trivial and unfocused. These openings can provide energy and momentum for reading.

We can take as an example the opening to a classic paper by psychologists Roger Brown and James Kulik, cited over a thousand times, that introduced the concept of "flashbulb memories." The paper explores the way we keep something like a photographic memory of key events (like the collapse of the World Trade Centers), retaining even seemingly trivial details about where we were when we heard the news—apparently a universal phenomenon. The paper, published in the journal *Cognition*, begins this way:

> *"Hardly a man is now alive" who cannot recall the circumstances in which he heard that John Kennedy had been shot in Dallas. Not just the fact that John Kennedy had been shot and died; we remember that too, of course, but we really do not need to since it is recorded in countless places and in many forms. It is not the memory of the event that invites inquiry, but the memory of one's own circumstances on first hearing the news. There is no obvious utility in such memories.* (1977, 73)

The last line of this opening established the dramatic tension of the paper—that we hold these specific memories of how we learned about these momentous events, but there is no obvious utility in retaining this specific information. Why have we evolved to use our limited memory capacity to hold on to this information? The paper takes on the structure of a quest, an exploration or inquiry that gives it real momentum.

Academic arguments are situated in a context and take "form" in the sense Burke (1968) describes it—"an arousing and fulfillment of desire." At their best, they create curiosity, anticipation, even suspense. In fact, some have argued that the "problem-finding" part of investigation is at least as important as the problem-solving part. In their book *The Creative Vision*, Jacob Getzels and Mihaly Csikszentmihalyi (1976) introduce this concept to the discussion of how creative artists work. The mind-set they describe is something more than the familiar concept of *problem solving*, where the learner is presented with defined difficulty to be resolved. They argue that:

> *Finding a problem, that is, functioning effectively in a discovered problem situation, may be a more important aspect of creative thinking and creative performance than in solving a problem once it has been found and formulated.* (82)

Albert Einstein and Leopold Infeld said something similar in their survey of major discoveries in physics: "The formulation of a problem is often more essential than its solution, which may merely be a matter of mathematical or experimental skill" (1938, 95). To be sure, there is the work of demonstration, claims and evidence and analysis, and this writing can fail when these are done poorly—but these exist in a macrostructure of narrative, a story of inquiry in the field. There is a plot, establishing a tension and a movement toward resolution. These claims exist in history, in time. And although the language itself may seem impersonal, even academics respond to the artfulness of construction, to form, to what I am calling "plot."

COUNTERDISCOURSE

Counterdiscourse involves the creating of opposition to any point the writer is making. It is inviting in an adversary, even creating one. It is asking, "How can it be otherwise?" Gretchen Bernabei calls it "jerk talk." Others, more elegantly, call it "inviting in a naysayer."

As teachers, we can pose as this other voice to model this critical thinking skill. We can say, "Suppose someone said this . . . about your idea, how would you respond?"

It takes a while before students can fully incorporate a range of viewpoints in their writing—but it is important to engage them with this kind of challenge. I say to my students, "Wherever you are, whatever your position is—I will be someplace different."

Imagining the viewpoint of those who disagree with you (and not simply dismissing and ignoring them) is the beginning of intellectual— and moral—maturity.

The process of problem finding might also be called "critical thinking," which everyone, of course, advocates—but it is not always clear what such thinking is critical *of*. There needs to be an object of the criticism. This object, I would argue, is routine, common sense, habit, superficiality, accepted wisdom, consensus, niceness, decorum, tradition, laziness. We open up a problem, when we break free of all this regulation, this deadweight, to find discrepant information, pursue anomalies, missed possibilities, and generate alternatives—"How could it be otherwise?" is the central question in critical thinking. The great French essayist Montaigne had many Latin expressions carved into the ceiling beams of his study—one was *iudicio alternante*: altering judgment or opinion, the necessity of an active mind to keep moving and never be fixed in one spot. As Kenneth Burke advised: "When in Rome, do as the Greeks" (1968, 119).

Critical thinking—playing with the drama of ideas, the orchestration of voices and positions—is the source of plot and movement in analytic writing. Not to get too dermatological, but it creates the itch to be scratched.

words

Let's be honest—we are somewhat embarrassed by this affection, this dependence on narrative. We can feel it is an indulgence, a lapse, a form of sentimentality. It is a desire for the easy way out, the verbal equivalent of a craving for sugar and fried food. If we were only more intellectually rigorous (we tell ourselves), we would rely solely on rationality, on data, on logical argument, on objectivity. We would be convinced by it. We wouldn't be so "anecdotal," so tied to emotional appeals.

But we are not made that way. At the end of a great poem, William Butler Yeats (1993) describes a shift in his poetry from the grand themes and mythology of his earlier work, to a more intimate kind of poetry:

> *Now that my ladder's gone*
> *I must lie down where all ladders start,*
> *In the foul rag and bone shop of the heart.*

Persuasion does business in this "foul rag and bone shop of the heart" (remember that the Latin root for "core" is "cor," meaning heart). If we are to prepare students for the world as it is—and not as we pretend it to be—we need to let them in on this secret.

NUMBERS THAT TELL A STORY

For now the signs were there for him to read; as he watched the new figures chalked up on the board, he read their meaning clearly, and once again, in advance of all the others in the crowded room, he sensed misfortune—this time not its possibility, but its confirmation.

EDWIN O'CONNOR, *THE LAST HURRAH*

The connection of narrative to mathematics, or to numerical information in general, is not immediately obvious. They seem to be different symbol systems, one language, one numbers. Yet even in Egyptian times, as early as 1600 BC mathematics was taught via story problem. Here is problem 79 from the Rhind Papyrus:

> *There are seven houses; in each house there are seven cats; each cat kills seven mice; each mouse has eaten seven grains of barley; each grain would have produced seven hekat. What is the sum of all the enumerated things?* (Mathematics Illuminated, Egypt and India)

And how can any of us forget all those trains hurtling toward each other at different speeds, leading to an episode on *The Simpsons* (1994) where Bart riffs on the classic train problem while taking an aptitude test. As he contemplates an insanely complicated problem featuring two trains barreling toward each other, he gets anxious and starts chewing his pencil.

His teacher, Mrs. Krabappel, urges him to visualize the problem, and Bart begins to see himself surrounded by numbers and trampled by passengers getting on and off the train—until the conductor wakes him from his dream.

This train scenario was undoubtedly overworked—even in my day there wasn't that much train travel, and I'm sure those who did travel were not so obsessed about trains meeting unless they were on the same track. But it was at least an attempt to embed mathematics in real-world situations and make it less abstract. It is one of many ways in which we rely on narrative to understand quantitative information.

Not only might the "problem" be presented in a story form, but the process of mathematical reasoning also has a story arc. Recall an earlier quotation from Burke that literary form is "an arousing and fulfillment of desire" (1968, 124). Now compare that formulation to this description of how "meaning" is sought in the process of mathematical reasoning, as described by the British math educator Leone Burton. She describes the "ebb and flow" of cognitive activity in three phases: entry, attack, and review.

> As meaning is sought, commitment is tentatively aroused. This phase of engaging is described as entry. Surprise, curiosity, or tension creates an affective need. To resolve this need requires further exploration that in turn satisfies the cognitive need to get a sense of the underlying pattern. . . . [T]here are two possible affective means of dealing with conflict. One is to engage further and attack the cause of the conflict. The other is to withdraw with a sense of failure and incapacity. Moving from the entry phase to attack and engaging is likely only in the person who is already aware of enough success from previous attacks for his or her confidence to cope with possibility of failure on this occasion. (1984, 41)

This process involves the manipulation of elements (a diagram, an equation, a picture) that can help the learner achieve a gratifying resolution, a "sense of pattern or connectedness" that "releases the tension into achievement, wonder, pleasure, or further surprise that drives the process on" (41). Although there are skills of manipulation that are specific to mathematics, this process, as Leone affirms, is not specific to mathematics; it is identical to the sense of plot that I attempted to define throughout this book.

The Process of Math Reasoning

It helps to explore this process in a concrete example that Leone provides. Although I'm sure that some of you went into literacy education to *avoid* problems like this, suppose we relax and take it a step at a time.

> *At a warehouse I was informed that I could obtain a 20% discount on my purchase but would have to pay a 15% sales tax. Which would be better for me to have calculated first, discount or tax?*
> (Burton 2004, 42)

First off, this seemed like a reasonable question that might arise in a purchase. My initial hunch was that it *would* make a difference, but which way was best? The simplest strategy I could figure was just to work out each option using a purchase of $100. So the tax-first approach went like this:

Step 1: $100 × 1.15 = $115 (I use the 1.15 to figure the amount rather than figuring the 15 percent tax and adding it—it saves me a step.)
Step 2: $115 × .8 = $92

Now the reverse order for discount first:

Step 1: $100 × .8 = $80
Step 2: $80 × 1.15 = $92

I'm surprised. No difference. So I wondered if I could dredge up some mathematical notation to demonstrate this. What happens if we let *a* equal *any* amount, and *remember you do the work on the parentheses first*:

Does .8 (*a* × 1.15) equal 1.15 (*a* × .8)?
.8 × 1.15*a* = 1.15 × .8*a*
.92 *a* = .92*a*

OK, clumsy, but this is a step forward: I have proved that with this discount and this tax, the order makes no difference, and the amount makes no difference; it works for any *a*. But is this a special case with this tax and this discount?

What happens if we change the discount and tax rates? Let's try a discount of 20 percent and a more American tax of 5 percent, keeping the purchase at 100:

So tax first: .8 (100 × 1.05) = .8 × 105
                              = 84

Discount first: $1.05 (100 \times .80) = 1.05 \times 80$
$$= 84$$

The order of multiplication doesn't matter; in mathematical terms it is a *combination* where the order doesn't matter. It doesn't matter in the sample case, or in any situation like this, no matter the cost, discount rate, or tax rate. This process is what Burton calls the pleasure in finding a pattern.

Jack Wilde Plays the Numbers and Other Stories

Algebra often comes at students as a set of numbers and symbols—which for many students is intimidating and overly abstract. Jack Wilde, a teacher in our summer program, argues that students need a context, even a metaphor, for learning algebra. He provides that context when he plays Number Machine with his fifth graders. It works like this.

He says to his students, "I'm a Number Machine. You give me a number and I change it by taking one action—multiplication, addition, division. Your job is to figure out the rule I'm using to do it. I'll keep doing it as long as you need me to. Here's a bag that I will call a. Put your numbers in it."

He'll pick a number—say a 2 and he'll say, "Eight." Well, there are two possibilities: he could have added 6 or multiplied the 2 by 4. He takes another number, this time 6, and gives back 12. Now the principle is clear: he adds 6 to the number: b (the number created by the machine) $= a + 6$.

After a few examples, he tells the students that the number machine is going to do two things to the a's, a multiplication and an addition (and to keep things simple we are dealing with positive whole numbers larger than 0). He takes out another number, 6, and comes up with 34. Now there are a lot of possibilities (multiply by 6 and subtract 2; multiply by 4 and add 10).

He takes another number, 10, and the machine comes up with 42. Now we know the multiplication number has to be less than 5 (because 10 times 5 is 50). There are only four options and it is easy to try out all of them, starting with one:

1—Doesn't work: $1 \times 6 + 28$ would $= 34$. But $1 \times 10 + 32$ would $= 42$. Couldn't be the same formula.
2—Paydirt: $2 \times 6 = 12 + 22 = 34$; $2 \times 10 + 22 = 42$.

So here's the equation the machine used: $b = 2a + 22$. I'm sure Jack's fifth graders came up with less clunky ways of doing this—I never claim to be as smart as a fifth grader. This approach is an inductive way of learning basic algebra—one built on the metaphor of the number machine.

As the number machine example shows, math becomes more accessible when it is embedded in a game—and games are a form of story. They have rules, challenge, suspense, and resolution.

Here is another example of creating a game-like story for learning graphing and measurement in second grade.

During one snowy year, a second-grade teacher in our district noticed in *The Boston Globe* a chart that showed the accumulation of snow as measured against an image of Robert Parish, the Celtic's seven-foot center. Parish, who stands 84.5 inches tall, was eclipsed by the 89.5 inches of snow.

As a variation, this teacher had her students trace a silhouette of Chuck Goebbel, the willing gym teacher (and one of the few males in the school), and alongside they measured out his height in feet and inches—then each person in the class guessed how much of Goebbel would be covered by snow. As with the *Globe*'s Parish, each time there was a snowfall, students would check the paper to see how much had fallen and they would cover him up that amount. Measurement is made concrete—and dramatic.

Stories in the Box Score— a First Data Set

If we were to identify a basic "life skill" task that crosses professions and disciplines, interpreting a data set would surely be high on a list. On the school board where I serve, we are inundated with spreadsheets that challenge us to makes sense of these numbers, to separate the signal from the noise. A good number sense is critical. Data sets will also be a feature on the newly designed SAT tests (Lewin 2013, 16). How do we translate numbers into meaningful patterns—how do they tell a story? How do they invite us to speculate on causes and predict future actions?

For my son—and me—this affection for numbers began with baseball. We share a love for box scores and can use them to reconstruct games, and it fostered a love of numbers that he retains to this day. In fact, I believe (with no evidence, mind you) that one traditional advantage boys have had in math is their early acquaintance with sports statistics, particularly baseball. We were introduced to decimals, as batting averages, before we knew what a decimal was.

I recall seeing the box score for a Boston Red Sox loss to the Baltimore Orioles around the midpoint of their 2013 (championship) season. It tells a story to the careful reader, beginning with the score, 2–0, an unusually small number of runs. So, what gives? One piece of information jumps out. *Three stinking hits* over a whole game for the Red Sox, and none from the heart of the line-up (hitters three, four, and five). And a wasted effort by the Sox pitcher, Ryan Dempster, who worked into the eighth inning (rare these days) and gave up only two runs and six hits.

We can also get a flavor of Dempster's pitching performance from one interesting number, Baltimore's performance with men in scoring position (i.e., on second or third base). They were one for twelve, an abysmal number, indicating that Dempster had to regularly pitch out of difficulty (his five walks contribute), and Baltimore hitters really failed when they could have been scoring. The Red Sox were little better in the clutch—1-7, and that hit wasn't enough to score a run, probably an infield hit by Iglesias with Karp on second. A frustrating evening for the beloved Red Sox, continuing their struggles against Baltimore. This is a kind of storytelling through numbers that sports nerds love.

If we think of the skills to read a data set, they are very similar to those for any form of reading. *Prior knowledge* is critical for establishing a set of norms or expectations. When these norms are violated, we are suddenly alert to the unusual situation we find ourselves in. Something interesting is happening.

Similarly, in the case of the Red Sox box score, anyone knowledgeable about baseball knows that a team usually has about nine hits in a game— so three hits represents a deviation, an interesting anomaly. It has "surprise value." This disruption of the normal pattern can lead to an investigation of the cause, the failure of the key part of the lineup, and to pose further questions to consider: has the heart of the lineup been producing? Should it be shaken up? Or is this just a one-time occurrence? All of which call for more data sets. This is active, recursive, critical reading, what John Dewey called *intelligence*.

Reading a data set for surprising information can also be a great pleasure—even a perverse delight in challenging common wisdom, in disrupting the accepted narrative. We can counter a tendency that Daniel Kahneman (2011) calls the "availability" effect: that is, we regularly take whatever information is most readily available and generalize from it. The shootings at Newtown, Connecticut created the vivid impression that schools were becoming more dangerous places. School districts like my

Percentage of students ages 12–18 who reported criminal victimization at school during the previous 6 months, by type of victimization and selected student characteristics: 1999, 2005, and 2009											
	1999				2005				2009			
Student characteristic	Total	Theft	Violent	Serious violent	Total	Theft	Violent	Serious violent	Total	Theft	Violent	Serious violent
Total	7.6	5.7	2.3	0.5	4.3	3.1	1.2	0.3	3.9	2.8	1.4	0.3
Sex												
Male	7.8	5.7	2.5	0.6	4.6	3.1	1.6	0.3	4.6	3.4	1.6	0.6
Female	7.3	5.7	2.0	0.5	3.9	3.2	0.8	0.3	3.2	2.1	1.1	

Figure 8.1 Indicators of School Crime and Safety, 2011
(Robers, Zhang, and Truman 2012)

own immediately spent considerable funds on entryway cameras and other safety measures.

But in fact, schools have become dramatically safer in the past fifteen years, with violent crime in 2009 at 60 percent of the 1999 figure—actually a good news story. And other data show that when students leave home for school, they are, on average, going to a much safer place (see Figure 8.1). The increase in violent video games caused many people to believe that it is responsible for more violent behavior among boys, when, in fact, youth violence has declined during the same period.

As another example, the general public "knows" our school system is in precarious decline, in crisis: yet reading scores have risen over the past decade according to the National Assessment of Educational Progress. This illustrates another point Kahneman makes, that the simple repetition of a claim, like the "crisis" in American education, can lead to it being accepted as a fact. But data can puncture comfortable myths and create alternative narratives, counternarratives—indeed some like Steven Levitt and Stephen Dubner (2005), of "freakonomics" fame, have made a career of it.

So let's try a little freakonomics on the data set that follows, which I consulted a few years ago when I was writing an encyclopedia piece on the baby boom. We all know the story: birthrates were low during the war because so many men were off to the war, and when they returned the rate skyrocketed as they all began to have families; in fact, that's my own story, as I was on the early end of this boom.

But the numbers tell a somewhat different story.

Birthrates (and percentage of marriages) declined in the Great Depression years, suggesting that they were tied closely to the economic distress

YEAR	NUMBER (1,000)					RATE PER 1,000 POPULATION				
	Births	Deaths		Marriages	Divorces	Births	Deaths		Marriages	Divorces
		Total	Infant				Total	Infant		
1910	2,777	697	(NA)	948	83	30.1	14.7	(NA)	10.3	.9
1915	2,965	816	78	1,008	104	29.5	13.2	99.9	10.0	1.0
1920	2,950	1,118	130	1,274	171	27.7	13.0	85.8	12.0	1.6
1925	2,909	1,192	135	1,188	176	25.1	11.7	71.7	10.3	1.5
1930	2,618	1,327	142	1,127	196	21.3	11.3	64.6	9.2	1.6
1935	2,377	1,393	120	1,327	218	18.7	10.9	55.7	10.4	1.7
1940	2,559	1,417	111	1,596	264	19.4	10.8	47.0	12.1	2.0
1945	2,858	1,402	105	1,613	485	20.4	10.6	38.3	12.2	3.5
1950	3,632	1,452	104	1,667	385	24.1	9.6	29.2	11.1	2.6
1955	4,097	1,529	107	1,531	377	25.0	9.3	26.4	9.3	2.3
1960	4,258	1,712	111	1,523	393	23.7	9.5	26.0	8.5	2.2
1962	4,167	1,757	105	1,577	413	22.4	9.5	25.3	8.5	2.2
1963	4,098	1,814	103	1,654	428	21.7	9.6	25.2	8.8	2.3
1964	4,027	1,798	100	1,725	450	21.0	9.4	24.8	9.0	2.4
1965	3,760	1,828	93	1,800	479	19.4	9.4	24.7	9.3	2.5
1966	3,606	1,863	86	1,857	499	18.4	9.5	23.7	9.5	2.5
1967	3,521	1,851	79	1,927	523	17.8	9.4	22.4	9.7	2.6
1968	3,502	1,930	76	2,069	584	17.5	9.7	21.8	10.4	2.9
1969	3,600	1,922	75	2,145	639	17.8	9.5	20.7	10.6	3.2
1970	3,731	1,921	75	2,159	708	18.4	9.5	20.0	10.6	3.5
1971	3,556	1,928	68	2,190	773	17.2	9.3	19.1	10.6	3.7
1972	3,258	1,964	60	2,282	845	15.6	9.4	18.5	11.0	4.1
1973	3,137	1,973	56	2,284	915	14.9	9.4	17.7	10.9	4.4
1974	3,160	1,934	53	2,230	977	14.9	9.2	16.7	10.5	4.6
1975	3,144	1,893	51	2,153	1,036	14.8	8.8	16.1	10.1	4.9
1976	3,168	1,909	48	2,155	1,083	14.8	8.9	15.2	10.0	5.0
1977	3,327	1,900	47	2,178	1,091	15.4	8.8	14.1	10.1	5.0
1978	3,333	1,928	46	2,282	1,130	15.3	8.8	13.8	10.5	5.2
1979, prel.	3,473	1,906	45	2,359	1,170	15.8	8.7	13.0	10.7	5.3

Figure 8.2 U.S. Birthrates, 1910–1979 (U.S. Bureau of the Census 1980)

of the times, but *went up* during the war years, even with so many men deployed. In 1945, the peak time of deployment, there were 20.4 births/1,000 population, compared to 18.7 in 1935 when the U.S. army was miniscule (see Figure 8.2).

So did the birthrate *boom*? It did go up to its highest point in 1955 with 25.0 births. More precise, year-by-year data would show a spike to about 26 in 1947 (the year before I was born)—leading to building two elementary schools in our small town. But by 1975 it had dropped substantially: *at 14.8, it was 72 percent of the birthrate during the war years*. Even in 1965, just ten years after the peak year on the chart, the rate was lower than in the last year of the war. Other data from the census, not on this chart, show it declining to a low of 13.9 in 2002.

So what can we conclude? There was a "boom" after the war. But there was a *steady decline* after that. We can conclude that there are *two* real reasons for the demographic bulge known as the baby boom—yes, there was an increase in births after the war, though a lot of babies were born *during* the war, more than I expected. But there has been an equally dramatic decline after that peak, as baby boomers chose to have much smaller families. There was a "baby bust."

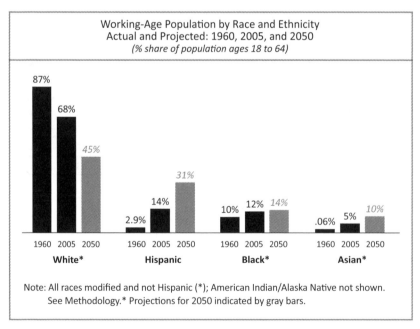

Figure 8.3 Working-Age Population by Race and Ethnicity

If we dig deeper into the census data, looking at the changes in birthrates among different racial groups, we get an even more revealing pattern of birthrate changes. In the period after the war, whites were a big majority of the population; in 1960 they made up 87 percent of those between eighteen and sixty-four—so the peak 25.0 fertility rate was reflective of white families. But by 2008, the birthrate for white families was down to 11.3, only 45 percent of the 1955 U.S. rate. By contrast, the Hispanic birthrate in 2008 was 22.2 (close to the baby boom numbers of the 1950s). All of which leads to charts like the one in Figure 8.3 (now there's a chart that tells a story) that project major shifts in the U.S. population and show that whites will make up a minority of the working-age population in 2050. Looking to the future, we might predict a number of cultural and political changes based on these numbers.

- Some members of the Republican Party have already decided that there is no future in demonizing immigrants. In general, an election strategy that appeals to whites exclusively will fail.
- Predominantly "white" states will lose political power to states like Texas, Arizona, and California with growing Hispanic and Asian population—already underway.
- There will be a Hispanic president within the lifetimes of our students.
- All U.S. students will be expected to learn more about Hispanic culture, literature, and history. That is, the English curriculum will no longer have the American/British literature division. *One Hundred Years of Solitude* (1970) will be part of the core curriculum.
- The ability to speak Spanish will be a key, even required, job asset.

In sum, these data sets tell a story of our country, particularly as we put into play multiple variables—time, ethnicity, and birthrate.

The Visual Display of Quantitative Information

Data sets are regularly turned into graphs and charts that display quantitative information. The acknowledged Godfather of visual information is Edward Tufte, author of the elegant and groundbreaking book *The Visual Display of Quantitative Information* (2001), and subsequent books that elaborate the artful and effective presentation of information—*Beautiful*

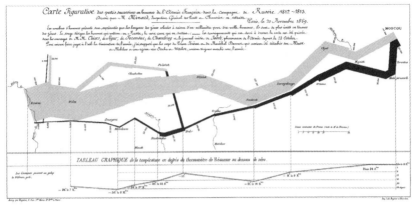

Reprinted by permission, Edward R. Tufte, *The Visual Display of Quantitative Information* (Cheshire, Connecticut, Graphics Press LLC, 1983, 2001).

Figure 8.4 Napoleon's March to Moscow

Evidence (2006), *Visual Explanations* (1997), and *Envisioning Information* (1990). Tufte returns, again and again, to Charles Minard's map that shows the decimation of Napoleon's army during the 1812 invasion of Russia. He claims that it "may well be the best statistical graphic ever drawn" (2001, 40). It plots six variables: the size of the army, its location on a two-dimensional surface (longitude and latitude), the direction of the army's movement, temperatures, and dates (Figure 8.4). Great graphics like this one are rich in information, integrating multiple data sets, inviting the reader to contemplate relationships and causality—in the case of Minard's graphic, we can imagine the toll that the frigid weather took, dropping to −30 degrees Celsius (−22 degrees Fahrenheit), as the army retreated through Poland.

Figure 8.5 would seem to fit Tufte's prescription (though he would be critical of the faint dotted lines, which provide key information). It integrates a fifty-seven-year time span, showing percentage of the British population that smokes, incidence of lung cancer, and gender—four variables that make for rich sets of relationships.

We can see the gender gap in smoking (the dotted lines) after the war, which decreased from about 25 percent in 1948 to about 3 percent in 2005. We can also see a decline in both men and women's smoking, starting about 1969. The decline in men's smoking corresponds to a decline in lung cancer incidence, dropping from about 116/100,000 to 60.

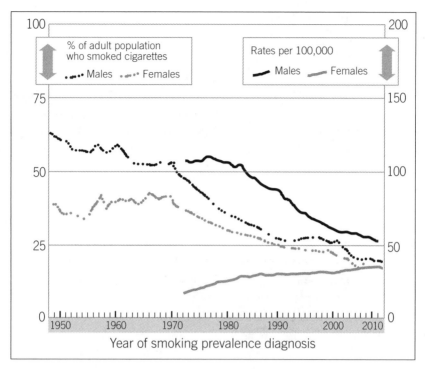

Figure 8.5 Lung Cancer Incidence and Smoking Trends

	1949	1959	1969	1979	1990	2000	2010	2011	2012
Men	14.1	18.4	18.9	21.6	16.8	15	14	13	12
Women	6.8	11.0	13.7	16.6	13.9	13	12	12	11

Figure 8.6 Daily Consumption of Manufactured Cigarettes per Smoker

Curiously the women's cancer incidence went up, which causes one to wonder if the average women began smoking more frequently, so that even if the percentage went down, the level of use went up—which turns out to be true (see Figure 8.6).

By 1969 the average female smoker was smoking twice as many cigarettes as were smoked in 1949, very likely leading to the rising rate of cancer in the 1970s through the 1990s. This rise in the number of cigarettes smoked by females coincides with special advertising claims—and products—aimed at women, most famously Virginia Slims ("You've come a long way, baby"). Collectively these charts tell a story of cultural change and medical history.

For some, these graphs and tables may seem like artifacts of the past, as technology and digital capacity allow for more complex and interactive displays of information (though I would still argue for teaching students to read them). But the advance is dazzling. Take, for example, a map created by an organization called Educational Experiences that shows life expectancies in the United States, county by county. Amazingly, it looks like a map of the divisions in the Civil War, with southern states having a much lower expectancy, especially for males.

I randomly click on a county in rural Mississippi, Attala County, where men live on average to 68.7 years, a bare three years beyond my own age. Curious, I compare it with my own county, Strafford in New Hampshire, 76.9, a difference of 8.3 years. I speculate that men live longest in the rich California communities around San Francisco (longevity correlates with wealth) and find that to be true, with Marin County having an average of 81.6—13 years longer than Attala in Mississippi.

With a single click, from male to female, the colors of the map dramatically change, though the Civil War pattern is still apparent. Where there are only a few counties in the entire country where men live on average to 80, it appears the norm for women. So what happens if I do the Attala-Strafford-Marin comparison for women? It goes:

Attala, Mississippi—77.1

Strafford, New Hampshire—81.4

Marin, California—85.1
(Institute for Health Metrics and Evaluation 2009a)

Significant but not so dramatic. And as Tufte has claimed, data sets like this provoke us to ask questions about causality—what is it in the lifestyles of these rural Mississippi men that so dramatically shortens their lives? Diet? Violence? Disease? Obesity? How does the racial make-up of the county correlate with longevity? And why do they seem to be more affected than women?

It turns out that as a state, Mississippi ranks second in the country in obesity rates (Louisiana is first)—so there is a likely connection there (Overweight and Obesity) (Institute for Health Metrics and Evaluation 2009b). Similarly, the male diabetes rates in some rural Mississippi counties approaches 20 percent, compared to about 7 percent in some suburbs of San Francisco (Diabetes Prevalence)—so we can infer that the lives of many of these Mississippi men are shortened by chronic diabetes.

We get an even more dramatic use of media and data in the amazing visual demonstrations created by Kevin Quealy and Graham Roberts (2012) for *The New York Times*. They have created a virtual race in which all the Olympic medalists in the 100-meter dash are running against each other, from Thomas Burke who won in the first modern Olympics in Athens in 1896 with a time of 12 seconds to Usian Bolt who won in 2008 and in 2012 with a record time of 9.69 (Burke would be sixty feet behind Bolt).

As we move back in time, we can see the greatest sprinters of all time— Carl Lewis, Jim Hines, Jesse Owens. We can see the dominance of the United States in the race, with challenges from England and more recently Jamaica. Quealy and Roberts then superimpose the relative positions of current U.S. age group champions; the fastest fifteen- to sixteen-year-old would have matched the bronze medal time in 1980. Not much of a sprinter myself, my own high school time would have kept me competitive in the first Olympics.

Then, in a brilliant twist, at the end of their presentation, they present a wide-angle view of all these one hundred runners, and scanning through them all shows the actual time difference over the 116 years of the race— 3.3 seconds from 1896 to the present. They all would have finished within that 3.3 seconds, as would I. An amazing amount of information, a graphic history of the race, all in less than three minutes.

When Information Becomes Art

In this book, I have tried to argue that the lines we draw between art and information are profoundly misguided. For it is by means of artfulness that we comprehend best. In effect, we can become prisoners of our own terminology. With the increased capacity to represent data visually, art and information, comprehension and sensuality merge. And nowhere more compellingly than in the work of two information specialists working for Google—Fernanda B. Viegas and Martin Wattenberg. Their mission is to create visual designs that enable viewers to experience data in a deeply personal and emotional way: "Our work explores the joy of revelation: the special electricity of seeing a city from the air, of hearing a secret, of watching a lover undress" (hint.fm, n.d.).

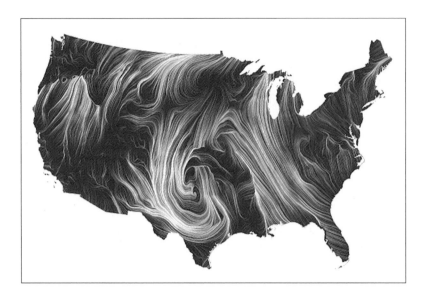

Figure 8.7 Google Wind Map

This invitation is irresistible when viewing their best known creation, "Wind Map" (Figure 8.7). At one glance the viewer can see all the wind currents in the United States—direction, location, wind speed, a network of lines and movements, a flow of activity, the country breathing. You can watch the winds swirl around Denver—and it suddenly makes sense why it is such an adventure to fly there. You can see the updrafts in the central prairie states and the dead calm of the current Northeast, in the middle of a heat wave. You can click to zoom in to watch a slow circuit of wind moving clockwise from Chicago, south toward Indianapolis, around to Kansas City, and back—or the steady east-to-west winds blowing across Texas (at a steady seven miles per hour). Strands of wind separate, combine, and swirl in the Rocky Mountains. It looks like a body, a circulatory system, an organism. It's mesmerizing; we experience the "joy of revelation" as data becomes visual patterns, as numbers become stories, even art.

> *As proponents of expressive visualization, we exploit the power of color and complexity to reveal arresting, unintuitive patterns. Parallel to depth of information, clarity and interactivity are of great concern to us. We strive to build intelligible visualizations that engage viewers at a formal level while allowing them to hold a dialogue with the underlying data. It is in this dialogue, we hope, that the brightest sparks of revelation will be found.* (hint.fm, n.d.)

In his TED talk, the noted math educator Dan Meyer has this lament:

> *Please imagine a time when you really loved something—a movie, an album, a song or a book—and you recommended it wholeheartedly to someone you also really liked. And you anticipated their reaction—and they hated it. So by way of introduction, that's the same state in which I've spent every working day for the last six years. I teach high school math. I sell a product to a market that doesn't want it, but is forced by law to buy it. It's just a losing proposition.* (2010)

This alienation from math is real, and a real concern if students are to move toward math-rich disciplines. And I suspect that a huge reason for this alienation is the disconnect between math as a tool in living authentic situations—and math as experienced in school. My own memory is of endless problem sets with small variations, and my lack of attention would lead to small, defeating errors. It involved so much plugging given information into formulas (Meyer asks, "In how many real situations do we have the exact information we need?"). The bright spot for me was anything to do with probability, which made instant sense to me because I could connect it to an affection for betting, for figuring odds.

Again, the baseball connection helped. To liven things up, my dad would make stupid bets with us. We might be watching an Indians-Yankees game and he would say, "A quarter that Moose Skowron will hit a home run." I'd take the bet, knowing the odds (about 35–1) were in my favor.

Meyer and many other reformers in the field argue for a more patient—and less cluttered—form of inquiry, one that follows an arc of experience, with problems that provoke mathematical reasoning. He works to resist the "just give me the formula" mentality that he sees in students and encourages an "attitude of suspended conclusion," a willingness to be puzzled, to formulate a problem, and seek tools and information to solve it.

It may also require the capacity of wonder, of awe. Math educator (and novelist) Manil Suri claims that we lose sight of the ideas of math such as the connection between polygons and circles:

> *Gaze at a sequence of regular polygons: a hexagon, an octagon, a decagon, and so on. I can almost imagine a yoga instructor asking a*

class to meditate on what would happen if the number of sides kept increasing indefinitely. Eventually, the sides shrink so much that the kinks start flattening out and the perimeter begins to appear curved. And then you see it: what will emerge is a circle, while at the same time the polygon can never actually become one. The realization is exhilarating—it lights up the pleasure centers of your brain. (2013)

This is math as drama, as story, the tension between the finite and the infinite.

It may be a stretch to call this narrative thinking, but narratives embed problems in human situations; and it is through a process of formulation, entry, tension, resolution—a plot—that we work through problems and transformations. Dewey claimed that the act of thinking, with its narrative arc, can be artful or aesthetic: "the experience itself has a satisfying emotional quality because it possesses internal organization and fulfillment through ordered and organized movement" (1934, 38).

And when this process works well we call it "elegant," and we call a mind skilled at this process—"beautiful."

CH 9

SPACE, RIGOR, AND TIME

Or, Our Metaphors Really Matter

The mind is not a vessel that needs filling, but wood that needs igniting.

PLUTARCH, "ON LISTENING TO LECTURES"

 hold before me the September 11, 2013 issue of *Education Week* with a slick surrounding advertisement from Curriculum Associates for a product called Ready®. According to the testimonials in the advertisement, Ready provides a set of lessons aligned to the Common Core State Standards that has "teachers of more than one million students already raving." "Teachers grabbed them like candy bars."

I tried to imagine this language being used about doctors or lawyers, or any other profession ("Cardiologists are eating up 4-D imaging like Triscuits"). So, curious, I turned the page to get a sample of these lessons.

I came across three that gave me pause. Under the category "Key Ideas and Details in Informational Texts," there was the objective "Finding Main Ideas and Details." And under "Key Ideas and Details in Literary Text" were these two lessons: Lesson 7: Finding the Theme of a Story or Drama, and Lesson 8: Finding the Theme of a Poem.

What struck me in all of these was the use of the verb *find*. As I have argued throughout this book, metaphors matter—and in this case reveal the conception of reading that underlies a teaching approach. Reading becomes an act of location. Comprehension is a sort of treasure hunt, an act of extraction. And because these themes or key details preexist, because they are absolutely *there*, in the text, accurate assessment is possible. If I hide my dog's favorite toy in the yard—he either finds it or he doesn't. I can tell definitively. Because I hid it, I know where it is. (Note that the expression "hidden meaning" also uses that metaphor.) The writer-reader transaction is a game of hide-and-seek.

What we have is a metaphor of the text as a space, an expanse, a container in which key features exist. It is essentially the dominant metaphor of the publishers' guidelines developed by CCSS writers David Coleman (now President of The College Board) and Susan Pimentel. Funded by the Gates Foundation, these guidelines will be consequential in the development of textbook lessons and very likely items on standardized tests. Note the persistence of this metaphor of *finding* as they describe the reading process (Coleman and Pimental 2011):

> *"The criteria make plain that developing students' prowess at* **drawing knowledge from the text itself is the point of reading**.*"* (1)

> *"The standards and these criteria sharpen the focus on the close connection between comprehension of text and* **acquisition of knowledge**.*"* (1)

> *"Complex text is* **a rich repository** *of ideas, information, and experience which all readers should learn how to access."* (3)

> *"The standards strongly focus on students* **gathering** *evidence, knowledge, and insight from what they read."* (6)

> *"Close reading and* **gathering** *information from specific texts should be at the heart of classroom activities."* (9)

> *"Focusing on extended texts will enable students to develop the stamina and persistence they need to read* **and extract knowledge and insight from larger volumes of material**.*"* (15)

> *"Complex text is a* **rich repository** *. . ."* (15) (emphasis added)

The text is viewed here as some kind of territory in which "knowledge, evidence, and insight" preexist prior to any reading act. The job of the student is to locate and "gather" or "extract" or pull from a "repository." They clinch this metaphor when they emphasize that the reader should stay within the "four corners of the text." The reader is, in effect, fenced in.

This conception of reading is text-controlled, text-dominant—as the meaning is already *there*. I always felt this power imbalance when taking a standardized test, as if I had to fit in someone else's skin; I had to psyche out what some "they" felt was significant. I had to abandon my own pattern of attention, which normally serves me well.

Coleman and Pimentel have come in for some criticism concerning their advocacy of cold reading of complex texts (Snow 2013), but it seems to me the more basic question is about their conception of reading itself—the metaphoric story they tell. For it runs counter to a transactional or constructionist model of reading in which knowledge is *made* and not *gathered* (the difference is profound). From a transactional perspective, the text does not have a determinate theme, existing within its four corners—that theme arises in the experience of reading, an interaction between reader and text.

An example. Years ago, my son, age about eight, decided to watch a film version of *Macbeth* with me, maybe thinking it was an action movie, which it sort of was. He hung in there for quite a while. Later in the day, we met one of my graduate students, and I mentioned that we had watched *Macbeth* together and she asked him what he thought of it.

"Good," he said, "it's about these little boys who are killed."

"Little boys who are killed?" That's what Macbeth is about? Then I recalled one brief scene, a matter of seconds in the movie, where Macduff's children are killed. That *would* register with an eight-year-old, but I never would have picked it as a major event in the play—though as I considered it, this was the most heinous act in the play, the degraded boundary of Macbeth's ambition. I learned something from his response.

From a transactional perspective, the text is not a defined space in which meaning exists, to be found by the reader. Rather the act of reading is an experience, in time, shaped by the writer, but profoundly influenced by the prior knowledge, purposes, emotional responses, and acts of attention of the reader. We are *never* bound by the "four corners of the text." Meaning is made, not found.

Creators of the CCSS have taken to mock the question: "How does this poem make you feel?" But in fact feeling and reaction provide the motivation, the foundation for analysis. We unpack that feeling, search for the aspects of the text that provoked it. The very concept of form as I have stressed in this book involves appetites and expectations that are not purely rational—indeed, they are embodied. We *feel* a response to a text (or movie, or song) before we can analyze the features that produced it.

Our intentions and acts of attention shape what we see in a text—we simply can't take it all in. The Roman essayist Seneca may have put it best:

*There is nothing particularly surprising about this way which every-
one has of deriving material for his own individual interests from
identical subject matter. In one and the same meadow the cow looks
for grass, the dog for a hare, and the stork for a lizard.* (1969, 210)

Rigor Mortis

The rigidity of this "four corners of the text" approach—and its dismissal
of emotion—is clearly related to the concept of rigor. If there is a God term
for the reform movement, *rigor* is it. And I may be one of the few holdouts
who is uncomfortable with its prominence. (Vicki Vinton and Alfie Kohn
are notable exceptions.) To begin with a qualification: if by *rigor* we mean
perseverance, stamina, ability to work through difficulty and sustain what
John Dewey called an "attitude of suspended conclusion," who can deny
its value? Of course it is what we want. But the question remains—what
are the conditions that support this perseverance?

The term is derived from the Latin word *rigor*, which means stiffness,
inflexibility, even bodily contraction as in *rigor mortis*. In an intellectual
sense, it is associated with austerity, asceticism, and moral sternness. I realize that the current use of the term does not have to carry this etymological
baggage, but even in current discussions, some of this connotation is there.
To be rigorous is to consciously exert effort on tasks that may be disagree-
able and unpleasurable and to be sustained in this effort by a long-term
goal that it is leading toward.

So what's the problem with that?

In my view, it is a misreading of human motivation. Of course, we want
students to be able to persist in tasks. But in my experience those who do
persist do so because they find a way to love, or at least enjoy, what they
are doing—and don't feel that they are being rigorous. Here for example is
Annie Dillard on writing:

> *Writing a book is like rearing children—willpower has very little to
> do with it. If you have a little baby crying in the middle of the night,
> and if you depend only on willpower to get you out of bed to feed the
> baby, the baby will starve. You do it out of love. Willpower is a weak
> idea; love is strong. You don't have to scourge yourself with a cat-o'-
> nine tails to go to the baby. You go to the baby out of love for that par-
> ticular baby. That's the same way you go to your desk.* (1987, 75–6)

This quote has always resonated with me. I particularly recall the day I finished writing *Misreading Masculinity: Boys, Literacy, and Popular Culture* (2002). I recall the time and place when I wrote the last sentence. Though there would be the inevitable steps of revision and copyediting, I knew I was basically done. And rather than feeling relief, I felt loss, as if a good friend was leaving town for good. I was losing a companion. I would no longer have those mornings where I would sort out my reading, opinions, and life history to see what would happen with the writing. My very capacity to persist in the project was due to this affection for what I was doing—never, on any day, to any sense that I was rigorous.

It is this affection, this caring, that can carry us forward to revise, rework, in the impossible task of getting it right. We can take lessons from the writers we love and teach, from F. Scott Fitzgerald's revisions of *The Great Gatsby*, for example. This great book, however inspired, is the act of a workman—testing every sentence, revising to make the action move more quickly, cutting excess description, and playing with the action that helps us imagine character. Even his great and memorable ending was tinkered with. The last two paragraphs read:

> *Gatsby believed in the green light, the orgastic future that year by year recedes before us. It eluded us then, but that's no matter—tomorrow we will run faster, stretch out our arms farther. . . . And then one fine morning—*
>
> *So we beat on, boats against the current, borne back ceaselessly into the past.* (189)

I must admit the chills I felt in seeing this ending, handwritten in the careful cursive penmanship Fitzgerald mastered in his Minnesota grammar school (though he never was much good at spelling!). This brilliant ending is nearly the same as that in the original manuscript. But in the original it is "a boat against the current." The revision seems to include us all as *individual* boats, with our own specific dreams, all of us failing to reach the unattainable. We can only guess at his intention, but the plural "boats" gives the image a more isolating, lonely feel—all of us alone with our separate dreams. We may want to call this attention to detail "rigor," but I prefer to see it as an act of devotion and caring.

I had been lucky to have great mentors and models, near and remote, living and dead. For fifteen years, I lived across the street from Don Murray, Pulitzer Prize winner and lifelong student of the writing process. He shared his insights with anyone who expressed interest in writing: workers at the local bagel shop, high school students, custodians, plumbers.

Perhaps his greatest lesson for me was to "listen to the text." Don claimed that the evolving text could "inform," could suggest direction if the writer was receptive to it (and not too rigid or tied to a predetermined plan). The evolving text can be an active partner in the writing—if we enter a receptive, flexible state of mind. Sentence could suggest sentence, ideas could spin out in unanticipated ways as we "expected the unexpected." He had no patience for those writers who dwelt on the agonies of writing—if it's so very painful, he would say, they should find other work. He passed on a very appealing vision of composing—almost gamelike, with a repertoire of moves and not of fixed forms.

Rigor without pleasure is usually a losing proposition; it runs against human nature. Take the sad case of the exercise bicycle. In our town there is a "spring pickup" where residents can put out just about anything for the garbagemen to take: old furniture, lamps, sports equipment, rusting tools. And invariably, outside some house there will be an exercise bicycle. While the cleanup is underway, people in pickup trucks cruise the neighborhood and take items along the curb; it's not uncommon to have everything in front of your house gone by the time the town trucks come by.

So here is my theory. Someone, call her Alice, cruises by an exercise bike on the street, and says, "I need to lose a few pounds. I'll pick this up and start riding it every day. After all, it's free for the taking." She puts it in the back of her Suburban, takes it to her basement, and for about five days rides it regularly, then intermittently, then not at all. It is just too boring, isolating, repetitive. So about a year later, in front of *her* yard, you will find that exercise bike. I have this image of exercise bikes circulating across the country this way.

To persist she would have had to find a way to make it less like work, maybe if she was exercising with friends (or actually riding a real bike). The regular runners and swimmers and hikers and yoga people I know persist because they love the activity itself—not because it is "good for them." They would persist even if it wasn't.

As to rigor and being rigorous, I would argue that we are at our best when we don't feel the sensation of strain or struggle. We can take counsel from Montaigne. As one of the greatest readers of the late renaissance, his observations should be taken seriously:

If I come across difficult passages in my reading I never bite my nails over them; after making a charge or two I let them be. . . . I can do nothing without gaiety and too much intensity dazzles my judgment, making it sad and weary. My vision becomes confused and dissipated. I must tell it to withdraw and then make fresh glancing attacks. (1987, 458)

Montaigne is careful not to turn his reading into an act of drudgery and is willing to cut his losses when persistence becomes wearying (still he managed to read virtually all of classical Roman literature). To retain his sense of "gaiety," he couldn't allow himself to use up his energy on difficulty, for this concentrated, self-consciously rigorous activity has been shown to deplete glucose and quickly tire us out. Any author who assumes a reader will endlessly persist in complexity will not have big readership (note how many used books, particularly assigned texts, are marked only in the first chapter).

We do better at complex tasks if we enter them with a sense of lightness, not feeling tense or rigid or under stress. We make an inadvertent nod to meditation when we ask students to "take a deep breath" if they are experiencing difficulty. When I wrote *The Performance of Self in Student Writing* (1997), I would begin each writing day by playing Samuel Barber's lovely Adagio for Strings, which put me in a relaxed mental space that allowed me to begin writing. I had to get any feeling of rigor out of my body.

One of the most helpful pieces of advice I ever received came when I was a freshman at Oberlin during a seemingly endless full week of orientation. A psychology professor told us that a key part of studying was recognizing when your energy/attention level was used up—to persist beyond that point was often unproductive. Better to monitor your efficiency and take a break, then come back in a better state of mind. It is so easy, *so easy*, to shift into an inattentive drifting state, which is the true enemy of learning.

I have even applied that principle to hiking in the White Mountains. There is usually a point in any serious hike when the grade shifts, or becomes rocky and difficult. Suddenly I find myself getting out of breath, my legs getting heavy, I'm sweating more—even my balance seems off because of the fatigue. A competitive part of my brain urges me on—tough it out.

But I've learned to silence it. I stop, stop frequently if that's what I need to get my breath back. If, on some rock faces, this means I stop every fifty steps, I do it. I experience two beneficial consequences from this attention to fatigue. One is that by stopping I can enjoy the hike better since many of these steep sections are the most spectacular.

And I feel in control. Paradoxically I feel even powerful by stopping. If I can control my fatigue, I can hike anything. The same goes for reading: by monitoring our effectiveness, and not pushing beyond our limits, we can handle harder texts.

I am also reassured by my acceptance of approximation; it's OK to come close, to get most of it. (Even the word *approximation*—being proximate, close to—shows how seductive the metaphor of space is!) We can never comprehend fully, argue definitively, or say exactly what we intended to. Perfection is a bitch and not really the right goal anyway. To read is to misread—to translate someone else's words into our own, never a one-to-one transaction and often a messy one. We have blind spots, biases, odd associations, lazy patches. As writers there are always avenues of research or explorations we were too tired to travel—or the clock runs out and we had to finish. Even the act of writing is translation. The novelist Michael Cunningham puts it this way:

> *You have, for months or years, been walking around with the idea of a novel in your mind, and in your mind it's transcendent, it's brilliantly comic and howlingly tragic, it contains everything you know, and everything you can imagine, about human life on the planet earth. It is vast and mysterious and awe-inspiring. It is a cathedral made of fire.*
>
> *But even if the book in question turns out fairly well, it's never the book that you'd hoped to write. It's smaller than the book you'd hoped to write. It is an object, a collection of sentences, and it does not remotely resemble a cathedral made of fire.*
>
> *It feels, in short, like a rather inept translation of a mythical great work.* (2010)

As we read we provide another level of translation, maybe one more step away from the "cathedral made of fire."

We are also at our best when we feel an expanse of time before—so that we can "dwell" in a process, be fully present, so rare in the increasingly cluttered school day. I recently discovered a set of tapes that Donald Graves and Lucy Calkins made during their groundbreaking study of children's writing in the late 1970s; I have watched these tapes with teachers and they universally note the slower pace. Students in the study were regularly given time to answer questions, often to take two or three tries at them. Calkins was a deft interviewer often using what I call the "blank probe"—"Tell me more." Teachers and researchers do not jump in when a student has difficulty (and if they do, it is often to ask what the student is doing; they don't solve the problem). The message is: take your time, I'm listening. Take as much time as you need.

As I watch these, I was reminded of another great teacher, my friend Ellin Keene, who gives students the gift of time and expectation in her interactions. If a student says, "I don't know," she responds, "I know you don't, honey, but if you did what would you say?" This kind of timescape is especially critical for English language learners, who are often defeated and silenced by the need to be quick in classroom discussions.

There are few unqualified generalizations we can make about great teaching. But I will hazard this one: great teachers never look rushed, and they don't make their students feel rushed.

words

It is conventional to view narrative as a mode, a type of writing, often an easy one. When we rely on stories we are accused of being "anecdotal," not intellectually serious. We are told that on the job and in college, we do the hard stuff, the rigorous stuff; we analyze and make logical arguments. We don't tell stories.

But we do. We can't get away from it. Even the arguments we make are often about a version of story, or in the service of story, or in the form of a story. Evidence regularly serves to establish which story, which claim for causality, is most plausible. We critique a story by imagining another story. Informational texts regularly describe processes (evolution, the autoimmune system, photosynthesis, global warming) that take narrative form.

We are caught in time, caught in history. Or rather, history is the form we give to time. We experience our very existence as a progression through time. When my mother lost this capacity she thought she was losing her mind, her *self*. We rely on stories not merely for entertainment, but for explanation, meaning, self-understanding. We instinctively make connections of cause and effect, and always have. To deny the centrality of narrative is to deny our own nature. We seek the companionship of a narrator who maintains our attention, and perhaps affection. We are not made for objectivity and pure abstraction—for timelessness. We have "literary minds" that respond to plot, character, and details in all kinds of writing.

As the apostle Paul writes in First Corinthians, as humans we "see through a glass darkly," and only through salvation after death, outside of time, can we see truth "face-to-face," in its pure timelessness. Until then, we must live *in* time and proceed by indirection, by narrative.

Plato says something similar in his dialogue in *Phaedrus*, at the point where he attempts to describe the nature of the soul—the very heart of the dialogue. He admits it is "a theme of large and more than mortal discourse" and he chooses to describe it, unforgettably, in a "figure," an extended analogy, a story of the chariot and two horses. If we were godlike, he seems to say, we could dispense with metaphors and analogies and approximations; we could see the truth directly.

But as humans, as time-bound mortals, we must tell stories.

GLOSSARY OF KEY TERMS

Binding time—A term coined by Peter Elbow to describe the sensation of consecutiveness and forward motion in reading (and music, also a temporal experience). In describing musical form, Leonard Bernstein claims that form is the feeling of inevitability, as if on note, one section, *must* follow another. It is the feeling of being drawn forward, even of "flow," without a conscious effort to "pay attention."

Causality—The innate capacity to view the world as coherent and meaningful (and not random and unpredictable). We instinctively assign causes to occurrences in our lives; in fact, we can't prevent ourselves from doing so. We believe that certain actions have reliable and predictable consequences—a belief that gives us agency in our lives. Our accounts of causality regularly take the form of stories.

Extractive reading—This is a form of informational reading; in fact, it is often represented as the primary way in which we read for information. It involves a dipping in to pull facts from texts, without a sense of a continuous reading experience. Much of our reading on the Internet is extractive reading. Key words to indicate this type of reading are *finding, gathering, locating*.

Form—Form is *not* simply a static pattern that can be outlined; it is more dynamic than that. Reading is the act of moving through time, and form is the property of writing that creates this forward motion. It is "an arousing and fulfillment of desire," as Kenneth Burke famously described it. It is an embodied sensation—we *feel* the lack of form.

Narrative—The form that stories take, often referred to as a "mode." Although often used as synonymous with *story*, it is a more technical term. I argue that narrative is the "deep structure" of sustained writing (including informational and persuasive writing), as it accommodates the human need for anticipation and resolution. It is rooted in our innate need to ascribe causality to the activity of our lives—turning this activity into what John Dewey has termed "experience."

Narrator—Though usually thought of as a feature of fiction, all writing is, in a sense, *narrated*. By that I mean we do not confront reality "raw"; we are in the hands of a mediator, a teller, a guide. As readers, we attend best when that narrator is in some way present, even if the "I" is not used. We can sense the energy, engagement, humor of this narrator—and when none of these qualities are present, when "no one is home," we have difficulty maintaining attention.

Plot—The dynamic working out of the conflict or tension within a narrative. Often there is some form of contention or "trouble," perhaps with an antagonist and protagonist (even if these are only ideas), that is resolved in the narration. The classic description of plot is in Aristotle's *Poetics*.

Story—Pervasive genre of communication and comprehension, primarily oral but also written. It is ordered by time (though not rigidly) and has some dramatic form or plot.

Sustained reading—The subject of this book. It involves a "staying with" the writer as ideas are developed. Where extractive reading is basically formless, in sustained reading we are carried forward by the author's employment of form—the sense of problem and solution, anticipation and fulfillment.

REFERENCES

Ambrose, Stephen. 1996. *Undaunted Courage: Meriwether Lewis, Thomas Jefferson, and the Opening of the American West*. New York: Simon & Schuster.

Anderson, Kare. 2012. "5 Ways Storytelling Can Boost Participation and Performance." *Forbes*, August 18. www.forbes.com/sites /kareanderson/2012/08/18/5-ways-storytelling-can-boost -participation-and-performance

Andrews, Roy Chapman. 1953. *All About Dinosaurs*. New York: Random House.

Bartholomae, David. 1983. "Writing Assignments: Where Writing Begins." In *FORUM: Essays on Theory and Practice in the Teaching of Writing*, edited by Patricia Stock, 300–312. Portsmouth, NH: Boynton/Cook Publishers.

Bartholomae, David, and Anthony Petroski, eds. 2011. *Ways of Reading: An Anthology for Writers*. Boston, MA: Bedford/St. Martin's.

Bate, Jonathan. 2007. "The Mirror of Life: How Shakespeare Conquered the World." *Harpers*, April, 37.

Bawarshi, Anis. 2003. *Genre and the Invention of the Writer: Reconsidering the Place of Invention in Composition*. Logan, UT: Utah State University Press.

Bernabei, Gretchen. 2005. *Reviving the Essay: How to Teach Structure Without Formula*. Shoreham, VT: Discovery Press.

———. 2012. *The Story of My Thinking: Expository Writing Activities for 13 Teaching Situations*. Portsmouth, NH: Heinemann.

Biggs, Alton et al. 2007. *Biology*. New York: McGraw/Glencoe.

Boo, Katherine. 2012. *Behind the Beautiful Forevers: Life, Death, and Hope in a Mumbai Undercity*. New York: Random House.

Booth, Wayne. 1961. *The Rhetoric of Fiction*. Chicago: University of Chicago Press.

———. 1963. "The Rhetorical Stance." *College Composition and Communication* 14(3): 139–45.

Borges, Jorge Luis. 1953. "El Idoma Analitico De John Wilkins." In *Oras Inquisiciones*. Buenos Aires: Emece.

Brooks, David. 2014. "The Refiner's Fire." *New York Times*, February 14. www.nytimes.com/2014/02/14/opinion/brooks-the-refiners-fire .html?_r=0

Brown, Roger, and James Kulik. 1977. "Flashbulb Memories." *Cognition* 5: 73–99.

Buell, Lawrence. 1995. *The Environmental Imagination: Thoreau, Nature Writing, and the Formation of American Culture.* Cambridge, MA: Harvard University Press.

Burke, Kenneth. 1966. *Language as Symbolic Action: Essays on Life, Literature, and Method.* Berkeley, CA: University of California Press.

———. 1968. *Counter-Statement.* Berkeley, CA: University of California Press.

Burton, Leone. 1984. "Mathematical Thinking: The Struggle for Meaning." *Journal for Research in Mathematics Education* 15(1): 35–49.

Carle, Eric. 1991. *A House for Hermit Crab.* New York: Simon & Schuster.

Carr, Nicholas. 2008. "Is Google Making Us Stupid? What the Internet Is Doing to Our Brains." *Atlantic Monthly*, July 1. www.the atlantic.com/magazine/archive/2008/07/is-google-making-us -stupid/306868/

Charon, Rita. 2006. *Narrative Medicine: Honoring the Stories of Illness.* New York: Oxford University Press.

Cobb, Vicki. 2003. *I Face the Wind.* New York: HarperCollins.

Cohen, Rich. 2013. "Sugar Love (A Not So Sweet Story)." *National Geographic*, August, 78–97.

Coleman, David, and Susan Pimental. 2011. "Publishers' Criteria for the Common Core State Standards in English Language Arts and Literacy, Grades 3–12." www.corestandards.org/assets/Publishers _Criteria_for_3-12.pdf

Connors, Robert J. 1999. "The Rise and Fall of the Modes of Discourse." In *The Braddock Essays: 1975–1998*, edited by Lisa Ede, 110–21. Boston: Bedford/St. Martin's.

Cunningham, Michael. 2010. "Found in Translation." *The New York Times*, October 2. nytimes.com/2010/10/03/opinion/03cunningham .html?pagewanted=all

Curtis Jr., Charles P., and Ferris Greenslet, eds. 1945. *The Practical Cogitator.* Boston: Houghton Mifflin Harcourt.

Davidson, James West, Michael B. Stoff, and Herman J. Viola. 2003. *The American Nation.* Upper Saddle River, NJ: Prentice Hall.

De Kruif, Paul. (1926) 1996. *Microbe Hunters*. New York: Harvest Books.

De Pierris, Graciela, and Michael Friedman. 2013. "Kant and Hume on Causality." In *The Stanford Encyclopedia of Philosophy* edited by Edward N. Zalta. http://plato.stanford.edu/archives/win2013/entries/kant-hume-causality/

Denning, Stephen. 2011. *The Leader's Guide to Storytelling: Mastering the Art and Discipline of Business Narrative*. San Francisco: Jossey-Bass.

Dewey, John. 1910. *How We Think*. Boston: D.C. Heath.

———. 1934. *Art as Experience*. New York: Perigee Books.

———. 1971. *The School and Society & The Child and the Curriculum*. Chicago: University of Chicago Press.

Didion, Joan. 1979. *The White Album: Essays*. New York: Simon & Schuster.

Dillard, Annie. 1987. "To Fashion a Text." In *Inventing the Truth: The Art and Craft of Memoir*, edited by William Zinsser, 53–75. Boston: Houghton Mifflin Harcourt.

Drugan, Robert. C., John P. Christianson, Timothy A. Warner, and Stephen Kent. 2013. "Resilience in Shock and Swim Stress Models of Depression." *Frontiers of Behavioral Neuroscience* 7(14). www.ncbi.nlm.nih.gov/pmc/articles/PMC3584259/

Duke, Nell. 2004. "The Case for Informational Text." *Educational Leadership* 61(6): 40–44. www.ascd.org/publications/educational-leadership/mar04/vol61/num06/The-Case-for-Informational-Text.aspx

Durkheim, Emile. 2001. *The Elementary Forms of Religious Life*. Translated by Carol Cosman. New York: Oxford.

Early, Jessica, and Meredith DeCosta. 2012. *Real World Writing for Secondary Students*. New York: Teachers College Press.

Ehrenfield, Joan. 2012. "Rutgers Office for the Promotion of Women in Science, Engineering, and Mathematics." http://sciencewomen.rutgers.edu/node/290

Einstein, Albert and Leopold Infled. 1938. *The Evolution of Physics: From Early Concepts to Relativity and Quanta*. Cambridge, England: University of Cambridge Press.

Elbow, Peter. 2000. "The Shifting Relationships Between Speech and Writing." In *Everyone Can Write: Essays Toward a Hopeful Theory of Writing and Teaching Writing*, 149–67. New York: Oxford University Press.

———. 2012. *Vernacular Eloquence: What Speech Can Bring to Writing*. New York: Oxford University Press.

Emig. Janet. 1971. *The Composing Processes of Twelfth Graders*. Urbana, IL: National Council of Teachers of English.

Eubanks, Phillip. 2004. "Poetics and Narrativity: How Texts Tell Stories." In *What Writing Is and How It Does It*, edited by Charles Bazerman and Paul Prior, 33–56. Mahwah, NJ: Lawrence Erlbaum.

Fabre, Henri. (1913) 1964. *The Insect World*. Greenwich, CT: Fawcett.

Feiler, Bruce. 2013. "The Stories That Bind Us." *The New York Times*, March 15. www.nytimes.com/2013/03/17/fashion/the-family-stories-that -bind-us-this-life.html?pagewanted=all&_r=0

Firestein, Stuart. 2012. *Ignorance: How It Drives Science*. New York: Oxford University Press.

Fitzgerald, F. Scott. (1925) 2003. *The Great Gatsby*. The Authorized Text. New York: Scribners.

Fitzgerald, Frances. 1979. *America Revised*. New York: Vintage.

Fivush, Robyn et al. 2010. "The Making of Autobiographical Memory: Inter- sections of Culture, Narratives and Identity." *International Journal of Psychology* 46(5): 321–345.

Forster, E. M. 1956. *Aspects of the Novel*. New York: Mariner Books.

Gallagher, Kelly. n.d. "Building Deeper Readers and Writers." Article of the Week. http://kellygallagher.org/resources/articles.html

Ganz, Marshall. 2009. "Why Stories Matter." *Sojourners*, March. http://sojo .net/magazine/2009/03/why-stories-matter.

George, William T. 1989. *Box Turtle at Long Pond*. New York: HarperCollins.

Getzels, Jacob, and Mihaly Csikszentmihalyi. 1976. *The Creative Vision: A Longitudinal Study of Problem Finding in Art*. Hoboken, NJ: Wiley.

Gladwell, Malcolm. 2011. "The Treatment." In *The Best American Science and Nature Writing*, edited by Mary Roach, 157–75. New York: Mariner Books.

Goffman, Erving. 1961. *Asylums: Essays on the Social Situation of Mental Patients and Other Inmates*. New York: Doubleday.

Goodwin, Doris Kearns. 2005. *Team of Rivals: The Political Genius of Abra- ham Lincoln*. New York: Simon & Schuster.

Grady, Denise. 2011. "An Immune System Trained to Kill Cancer." *The New York Times*, September 12. www.nytimes.com/2011/09/13 /health/13gene.html?pagewanted=all

Graff, Gerald, and Cathy Birkenstein. 2007. *They Say/I Say: The Moves That Matter in Academic Writing*. New York: Norton.

Greenblatt, Miriam, and Peter S. Lemmo. 2001. *Human Heritage: A World History*. New York: Glencoe/McGraw Hill.

Groopman, Jerome. 1997. *The Measure of Our Days: A Spiritual Exploration of Illness*. New York: Penguin.

———. 2008. *How Doctors Think*. New York: Houghton Mifflin Harcourt.

———. 2013. "What Is Autism?" *The New York Times Review of Books*, June 6, 40–42.

Gruber, Peter. 2011. *Tell to Win: Connect, Persuade, and Triumph with the Hidden Power of Story*. New York: Random House.

Hakim, Joy. 2007. *Teaching Guide for The First Americans: Prehistory–1600*. New York: Oxford University Press.

Hammond, W. Dorsey, and Denise Nessel. 2012. *The Comprehension Experience: Engaging Readers Through Effective Inquiry and Discussion*. Portsmouth, NH: Heinemann.

Hawking, Stephen, and Leonard Mlodinow. 2011. In *The Best American Science and Nature Writing*, edited by Mary Roach, 186–90. New York: Mariner Books.

Hint.fm. n.d. "About." http://hint.fm/about/

The Holy Bible. 1952. Revised Standard Version. New York: Nelson.

Institute for Health Metrics and Evaluation. 2009a. "USA Life Expectancy." www.worldlifeexpectancy.com/usa/life-expectancy-by-county

———. 2009b. "Diabetes Prevalence by County (US) Maps." www.health metricsandevaluation.org/tools/data-visualization/diabetes -prevalence-county-us-maps#/overview/explore

James, William. (1907) 1954. "What Pragmatism Means." In *American Thought: Civil War to World War I*, edited by Perry Miller, 165–182. New York: Holt, Rinehart, and Winston.

———. 1958. *Talks to Teachers on Psychology: And to Students on Some of Life's Ideals*. New York: Norton.

Johnson, Ian. 2010. "Finding the Fact About Mao's Victims." NYR Blog, December 20. www.nybooks.com/blogs/nyrblog/2010/dec/20 /finding-facts-about-maos-victims/

Kahneman, Daniel. 2011. *Thinking, Fast and Slow*. New York: Farrar, Straus & Giroux.

Keene and Zimmermann. 2007. *Mosaic of Thought: The Power of Comprehension Strategy Instruction*. Portsmouth: Heinemann.

Kinneavy, James. 1971. *A Theory of Discourse: The Aims of Discourse*. Englewood Cliffs, NJ: Prentice Hall.

Klosterman, Chuck. 2010. "The Ethicist." *The New York Times Magazine*, January 10.

Kolbert, Elizabeth. 2012. "The Big Heat." The *New Yorker*, July 23. www
    .newyorker.com/talk/comment/2012/07/23/120723taco_talk_kolbert

Kristof, Nicholas. 2009. "If This Isn't Slavery, What Is?" *The New York Times*,
    January 3. www.nytimes.com/2009/01/04/opinion/04kristof
    .html?_r=0

Krugman, Paul. 2012. "The Blackmail Caucus." *The New York Times*,
    November 1. www.nytimes.com/2012/11/02/opinion/krugman-the
    -blackmail-caucus.html?_r=0

Krugman, Paul. 2014. "Salvation Gets Cheap." *The New York Times*, April 17.
    www.nytimes.com/2014/04/18/opinion/krugman-salvation-gets
    -cheap.html?ref=paulkrugman&assetType=nyt_now&_r=0

Lamstein, Sarah Marwil. 2010. *Big Night for Salamanders*. Honesdale, PA:
    Boyds Mills Press.

Leon, Jose A., and Gala E. Penalba. 2002. "Understanding Causality and
    Temporal Sequence in Scientific Discourse." In *The Psychology of
    Text Comprehension*, edited by Jose Otero, Jose A. Leon, and Arthur
    C. Graesser, 155–78. Mahwah, NJ: Lawrence Erlbaum.

Levinson, Cynthia. 2012. *We've Got a Job: The 1963 Birmingham Children's
    March*. New York: Scholastic.

Levitt, Steven D., and Stephen J. Dubner. 2005. *Freakonomics: A Rogue
    Economist Explores the Hidden Side of Everything*. New York:
    William Morrow.

Lewin, Tama. 2013. "Sneak Preview: What the New SAT and Digital ACT
    Might Look Like." *The New York Times*, August 4. www.nytimes
    .com/2013/08/04/education/edlife/what-the-new-sat-and-digital
    -act-might-look-like.html

Lindberg, Gary. 1986. "Coming to Words: Writing as Process and the
    Reading of Literature." In *Only Connect: Uniting Reading and Writing*,
    edited by Thomas Newkirk, 143–57. Upper Montclair, NJ: Boynton/
    Cook Publishers.

Linderholm, Tracy et al. 2000. "Effects of Casual Text Revisions on More-
    and Less-Skilled Readers' Comprehension of Easy and Difficult
    Texts." *Cognition and Instruction* 18(4): 525–56.

Lippincott. n.d. "Building Winning Brands in a Radically Transparent World."
    http://www.lippincott.com/files/documents/StoryExp_brochure.pdf

Macrorie, Ken. 1985. *Telling Writing*. 4th ed. Portsmouth, NH: Boynton/
    Cook Publishers.

Marcus, Ben. 2011. "What Have You Done?" *The New Yorker*, August 8, 55–63.

Markle, Sandra. 2004. *Polar Bears*. Minneapolis, MN: Carolrhoda Books.

Marquez, Gabriel Garcia. 1970. *One Hundred Years of Solitude*. New York: HarperCollins.

Maxwell, Richard, and Robert Dickman. 2007. *The Elements of Persuasion: Use Storytelling to Pitch Better, Sell Faster & Win More Business*. New York: HarperCollins.

McCullough, David. 2011. *John Adams*. New York: Simon & Schuster.

McPhee, John. 1968. *A Roomful of Hovings*. New York: Farrar, Straus & Giroux.

———. 1977. *Coming into the Country*. New York: Farrar, Straus & Giroux.

———. 1989. *The Control of Nature*. New York: Farrar, Straus & Giroux.

Medina, John. 2008. *Brain Rules: 12 Principles for Surviving and Thriving at Work, Home, and School*. Seattle: Pear Press.

Mencken, H. L. 1959. *A Mencken Chrestomathy*. New York: Knopf.

Meyer, Dan. 2010. "Math Class Needs a Makeover." www.ted.com/talks /dan_meyer_math_curriculum_makeover

Michotte, Albert. 1963. *The Perception of Causality*. Andover, MA: Methuen.

Moffett, James. 1968. *Teaching the Universe of Discourse*. Boston: Houghton Mifflin Harcourt.

Monmaney, Terence. 1993. "Marshall's Hunch." *The New Yorker*, September 20, 64–72.

Montaigne, Michel de. 1987. *The Complete Essays*. Translated by M. A. Screech. New York: Penguin.

Mooallem, Jon. 2011. "The Love That Dare Not Squack Its Name." In *The Best American Science and Nature Writing*, edited by Mary Roach, 243–62. New York: Mariner Books.

Moore, Lorrie. 1999. "Real Estate." In *Birds of America: Stories*. New York: Alfred A. Knopf.

Mukherjee, Siddhartha. 2010. *The Emperor of All Maladies: A Biography of Cancer*. New York: Scribner.

Murray, Donald. 2004. *The Craft of Revision*. 5th ed. Boston: Heinle.

Nabokov, Vladimir. 1955. *Lolita*. New York: Putnam.

National Dissemination Center for Children with Disabilities. 2011. "How People Read on the Web," August. nichcy.org/dissemination/tools /webwriting/reading

National Governors Association Center for Best Practices and Council of
    Chief State School Officers. 2010a. "Common Core State Standards
    for English Language Arts & Literacy in History/Social Studies,
    Science, and Technical Subjects." http://www.corestandards.org
    /ELA-Literacy/WHST/9-10/

———. 2010b. "Common Core State Standards for English Language Arts
    & Literacy in History/Social Studies, Science, and Technical Sub-
    jects: Appendix C." www.corestandards.org/assets/Appendix_C.pdf

———. 2010c. "Common Core State Standards for English Language Arts
    and Literacy in History/ Social Studies, Science, and Technical Sub-
    jects: Appendix A." www.corestandards.org/assets/Appendix_A.pdf

Newkirk, Thomas. 1989. *More Than Stories: The Range of Children's Writing*.
    Portsmouth, NH: Heinemann.

———. 1997. *The Performance of Self in Student Writing*. Portsmouth, NH:
    Boynton/Cook Publishers.

———. 2002. *Misreading Masculinity: Boys, Literacy, and Popular Culture*.
    Portsmouth, NH: Heinemann.

———. 2011. *The Art of Slow Reading: Six Time-Honored Practices for
    Engagement*. Portsmouth, NH: Heinemann.

Nijhuis, Michelle. 2013. "The Science and Art of Science Writing." *The New
    York Times*, December 9. http://opinionator.blogs.nytimes.com
    /author/michelle-nijhuis/

O'Connor, Edwin. 1956. *The Last Hurrah*. Boston: Little Brown.

Orwell, George. 2002. "Politics and the English Language." In *Essays*. New
    York: Albert A. Knopf.

Osnos, Evan. 2012. "Boss Rail." *The New Yorker*, October 22, 44–53.

Payne, Vaughn. (1965) 1969. *The Lively Art of Writing*. New York: Signet.

Pillemer, David. 1998. *Momentous Events, Vivid Memories*. Cambridge, MA:
    Harvard University Press.

Pitts, Jr., Leonard. 2012. "R-Rated Column, Not Suitable for New York's
    Kids." *Miami Herald*, March 31. www.miamiherald.com/2012
    /03/31/2723566/r-rated-column-not-suitable-for.html

Plato. 1990. "The Phaedrus." In *The Rhetorical Tradition: Readings from
    Classical Times to the Present*, edited by Patricia Bizzell and Bruce
    Hertzberg, 113–43. Boston, MA: Bedford/St. Martins.

Podgers, James. 2012. "The World of McElhaney." *ABA Journal*, October,
    32–39.

Poirier, Richard. 1997. "Reading Pragmatically." In *Pragmatism: A Reader*,
    edited by Louis Menand, 436–55. New York: Vintage.

Pollan, Michael. 2008. *In Defense of Food: An Eater's Manifesto*. New York: Penguin.

Pringle, Laurence. 1976. *Listen to the Crows*. New York: Thomas Y. Crowell.

Quealy, Kevin, and Graham Roberts. 2012. "All the Medalists: Men's 100-Meter Sprint." *The New York Times*. www.nytimes.com/interactive /2012/08/05/sports/olympics/the-100-meter-dash-one-race-every -medalist-ever.html?_r=0

Quinn, Jill Sisson. 2012. "Sign Here If You Exist." In *The Best American Science and Nature Writing, 2012*, edited by Mary Roach and Tim Folger, 274–90. Boston: Houghton Mifflin.

Rabinowitz, Peter. 1998. *Before Reading: Narrative Conventions and the Politics of Interpretation*. Columbus, OH: Ohio State University Press.

Rabinowitz, Peter, and Corinne Bancroft. 2014. "Euclid at the Core: Recentering Literary Education." *Style*. 47(1): 1–34.

Ravitch, Diane. 2003. *The Language Police: How Pressure Groups Restrict What Students Learn*. New York: Knopf.

Rosenblatt, Louise. 1994. *The Reader, the Text, and the Poem: The Transactional Theory of the Literary Work*. Carbondale, IL: University of Southern Illinois Press.

Robers, Simone, Jijun Zhang, and Jennifer Truman. 2012. "Indicators of School Crime and Safety: 2011." (NCES 2012-002/NCJ 236021). Washington, DC: National Center for Education Statistics, U.S. Department of Education, and Bureau of Justice Statistics, Office of Justice Programs, U.S. Department of Justice. http://www.bjs.gov /content/pub/pdf/iscs11.pdf

Sachs, Jonah. 2012. *Winning the Story Wars: Why Those Who Tell (and Live) the Best Stories Will Rule the Future*. Boston: Harvard Business Review Press.

Seligman, Martin. 1991. *Learned Optimism: How to Change Your Mind and Your Life*. New York: Knopf.

Seneca. 1969. *Letters from a Stoic*. New York: Penguin.

Simmons, Annette. 2007. *Whoever Tells the Best Story Wins: How to Use Your Own Stories to Communicate with Power and Impact*. New York: AMACOM Books.

Simon, Seymour. 1996. *The Heart: Our Circulatory System*. New York: HarperCollins.

The Simpsons. 1990. "Bart the Genius." Season 1, Episode 2: January 14. Fox. www.tv.com/shows/the-simpsons/bart-the-genius-1287/

Snow, Catherine. 2013. "Cold Versus Warm Close Reading: Stamina and the Accumulation of Misdirection." *Reading Today Online*, June 6. www .reading.org/general/Publications/blog/LRP/post/lrp/2013/06/06 /cold-versus-warm-close-reading-stamina-and-the-accumulation -of-misdirection

Suri, Manil. 2013. "How to Fall in Love with Math." *The New York Times*, September 15. www.nytimes.com/2013/09/16/opinion/how-to-fall -in-love-with-math.html

Taylor, Shelley. 1989. *Positive Illusions: Creative Self-Deception and the Healthy Mind*. New York: Basic Books.

Thomas, Lewis. 1974. *The Lives of a Cell: Notes of a Biology Watcher*. New York: Bantam.

Thoreau, Henry David. 1994. "Walking." In *The Art of the Personal Essay*, edited by Phillip Lopate, 480–505. New York: Anchor Books.

———. 2000. *Walden and Civil Disobedience*. Boston: Houghton Mifflin Harcourt.

Tiger, Lionel. 1979. *Optimism: The Biology of Hope*. New York: Kodansha.

Tough, Paul. 2012. *How Children Succeed: Grit, Curiosity, and the Hidden Power of Character*. Boston: Houghton Mifflin Harcourt.

Tufte, Edward R. 1990. *Envisioning Information*. Cheshire, CT: Graphics Press.

———. 1997. *Visual Explanations: Images and Quantities, Evidence and Narrative*. Cheshire, CT: Graphics Press.

———. 2001. *The Visual Display of Quantitative Information*. 2d ed. Cheshire, CT: Graphics Press.

———. 2006. *Beautiful Evidence*. Cheshire, CT: Graphics Press.

Tugend, Alina. 2013. "What It Takes to Make New College Graduates Employable." *The New York Times*, June 28. www.nytimes .com/2013/06/29/your-money/a-quest-to-make-college-graduates -employable.html?pagewanted=all

Turner, Mark. 1996. *The Literary Mind*. Oxford: Oxford University Press.

U.S. Bureau of the Census. 1980. *Statistical Abstract of the United States: 1980*. 101st ed. www2.census.gov/prod2/statcomp/documents /1980-01.pdf

Van den Broek, Paul et al. 2002. "Comprehension and Memory of Science Texts: Inferential Process and the Construction of a Mental Representation." In *The Psychology of Science Text Representation*, edited by Jose Otero, Jose Leon, and Arthur Graesser, 131–54. Mahwah, NJ: Lawrence Erlbaum.

Von Frisch, Karl. 1966. *The Dancing Bees: An Account of the Life and Sense of the Honey Bee*. Translated by Dora Isle and Norman Walker. New York: Harcourt Brace.

Williams, Joseph M. 1981. *Style: Ten Lessons in Clarity and Grace*. Glenview, IL: Scott Foresman.

Wills, Gary. 2006. *Lincoln at Gettysburg: Words That Remade America*. 2d ed. New York: Simon and Schuster.

Wilson, Timothy. 2011. *Redirect: The Surprising New Science of Psychological Change*. New York: Penguin.

Wordsworth, William. (1805) 1960. *The Prelude or Growth of a Poet's Mind*. London: Oxford University Press.

Yeats, William Butler. 1933. *The Collected Poems of William Butler Yeats*. New York: Macmillan.

Young, Jon. 2012. *What the Robin Knows: How Birds Reveal the Secrets of the Natural World*. Boston: Houghton Mifflin Harcourt.

Zemelman, Steve. 2011. "Common Core: Caution on Narrative Writing." Catalyst Chicago, November 7. www.catalyst-chicago.org /news/2011/11/07/common-core-wrongly-neglects-narrative -writing